WITHDRAWN

162 PICKETT *Manchester Valley*

# MASTERS OF POPULAR PAINTING

*Modern Primitives of Europe and America*

Text by Holger Cahill, Maximilien Gauthier,
Jean Cassou, Dorothy C. Miller and others

In collaboration with The Grenoble Museum

THE MUSEUM OF MODERN ART · NEW YORK

REPRINT EDITION, 1966 PUBLISHED FOR
THE MUSEUM OF MODERN ART BY ARNO PRESS

PRINTED IN THE UNITED STATES OF AMERICA

Reprint Edition 1966 Arno Press

*Library of Congress Catalog Card No. 66-26120*

# *Table of Contents*

## *Committee of Honor for the French Section*

M. le Ministre des Affaires Etrangères
M. le Ministre de l'Education Nationale
M. Georges Huisman, Directeur Général des Beaux-Arts
M. le Préfet de la Seine
M. le Président du Conseil Municipal de Paris
M. le Président de la Commission des Beaux-Arts de la Ville de Paris
M. le Président du Conseil Général de la Seine
M. le Président de la Commission des Beaux-Arts du Conseil Général de la Seine
M. Pierre Darras, Directeur des Beaux-Arts de la Ville de Paris
M. le Préfet de l'Isère, Grenoble
M. le Sénateur Léon Perrier, Président du Conseil Général de l'Isère, Grenoble
MM. les Sénateurs et Députés de l'Isère
M. le Recteur de l'Académie de Grenoble
M. Paul Cocat, Maire de Grenoble
La Municipalité et le Conseil Municipal de Grenoble
M. Keller, Président de la Chambre de Commerce de Grenoble
M. Henri Verne, Directeur des Musées Nationaux et de l'Ecole du Louvre
M. Jacques Jaujard, Sous-Directeur des Musées Nationaux et de l'Ecole du Louvre
M. Albert Henraux, Président de l'Association des Amis des Musées de France
M. Charles Pacquement, Président des Amis du Luxembourg
M. Julien Cain, Administrateur Général de la Bibliothèque Nationale
M. Roland Marcel, Commissaire Général du Tourisme, Paris
M. Paul Jamot, Membre de l'Institut, Conservateur Honoraire du Musée du Louvre
M. Raymond Escholier, Conservateur du Petit-Palais, Musée des Beaux-Arts de la Ville de Paris
M. René Huyghe, Conservateur du Département de la Peinture au Musée du Louvre

M. G.-H. Rivière, Conservateur du Musée National des Arts et Traditions Populaires

M. Louis Hautecoeur, Conservateur du Musée du Luxembourg

M. Robert Rey, Inspecteur Général des Musées de Province

M. Charles Montag, Délégué Suisse aux Expositions Francaises à l'Etranger

M. Anatole de Monzie, Président de la Société des Artistes Décorateurs

M. Edouard Herriot, Président du Salon des Tuileries

M. Maximilien Luce, Président du Salon des Indépendants

M. George Desvallières, Membre de l'Institut, Président du Salon d'Automne

M. Albert Sarraut, Président de la Commission de l'Exposition des Maîtres de l'Art Indépendant

M. Jean Cassou, Critique d'Art, Chargé de Mission au Cabinet de M. le Ministre de l'Education Nationale

Mlle. Eichmann, Critique d'Art à Prague

M. Vincenz Kramar, Conservateur du Musée de Prague

M. Jacques Guenne, Critique d'Art

M. Wilhelm Uhde, Critique d'Art

Princesse Bassiano, Amateur d'Art

M. F. Meyer, Amateur d'Art

Mme. Cécile Gregory, Amateur d'Art

M. André Paz, Amateur d'Art

M. Robert Delaunay, Artiste peintre

M. Henry Debraye, Archiviste Paléographe, Secrétaire Général de la Mairie de Grenoble

M. Maximilien Gauthier, Critique d'Art, Délégué à la Presse

M. Andry-Farcy, Conservateur du Musée de Grenoble

The European Section of the Exhibition (with the exception of the American loans) has been assembled under the direction of

M. ANDRY-FARCY, Director of the Grenoble Museum
*with the assistance of*
M. Maximilien Gauthier and
M. Henri Bing

# *Lenders to the Exhibition*

The names of several European lenders were not received in time for inclusion in the catalog.

Walter Abell, Brooklyn, New York
Edward N. Barnsley, Newtown, Pennsylvania
Mrs. Emile Branchard, New York
Mme. Jeanne Bucher, Paris
Dr. and Mrs. André Cournand, New York
Andrew Dasburg, Taos, New Mexico
Mr. and Mrs. Wendell Davis, New York
The Federal Art Project of the Works Progress Administration
Maximilien Gauthier, Paris
Mrs. Rose Gershwin, New York
Mme. Cécile Gregory, Paris
Miss Adelaide Milton de Groot, New York
Mrs. Edith G. Halpert, New York
Mr. and Mrs. William Averell Harriman, New York
Miss Cornelia Carle Hicks, Newtown, Pennsylvania
Mme. E. Hostettler
Thorvald Arenst Hoyer, Chicago
Peter Hunt, Provincetown, Massachusetts
R. Sturgis Ingersoll, Penlynn, Pennsylvania
Sidney Janis, New York
T. Catesby Jones, New York
The Adolph Lewisohn Collection, New York
Henry R. Luce, New York
Patrick Morgan, New York
Mr. and Mrs. William S. Paley, New York
Mrs. Charles S. Payson, New York
Horace Pippin, West Chester, Pennsylvania
Mrs. C. K. Post, New York
Mrs. John D. Rockefeller, Jr., New York
H. Leonard Simmons, New York
Robert H. Tannahill, Detroit, Michigan
Wilhelm Uhde, Paris
Max Weber, Great Neck, New York
E. Weyhe, New York
The American Folk Art Gallery, New York
Contemporary Arts, New York
Marie Harriman Gallery, New York
The Valentine Gallery, New York
The Walker Galleries, New York
The Weyhe Gallery, New York
The Grenoble Museum, Grenoble
The Newark Museum, Newark, New Jersey
Phillips Memorial Gallery, Washington, D. C.

# *Preface and Acknowledgment*

MASTERS OF POPULAR PAINTING is the third of a series of exhibitions outlined in 1933 and intended to present some of the major divisions or movements of modern art. The first, Cubism and Abstract Art, was held in the spring of 1936; the second, Fantastic Art, Dada and Surrealism, opened at the end of the same year. Both these exhibitions were sent on tour throughout the country.

As M. Cassou, M. Gauthier and Mr. Cahill point out in their essays, popular or folk art has always existed and during the past century it has been given increasing attention by students of national ethnography and social history. But it is only since the apotheosis of Henri Rousseau that *individual* popular artists have been taken seriously.

The purpose of this exhibition is to show, without apology or condescension, the paintings of some of these individuals, not as folk art, but as the work of painters of marked talent and consistently distinct personality. As a consequence of this program the vast body of anonymous "folk paintings" has not been represented at all.

Of the artists in the exhibition, Rousseau is of course the most famous in America as well as in Europe. Since his death almost thirty years ago he has had numerous exhibitions and fifteen or twenty of his paintings are already treasured by museums here and abroad. It has seemed wiser therefore not to attempt to show Rousseau at his full length at this time for the present exhibition is concerned primarily with his less renowned confreres.

Among the French constellation of popular artists, Bombois and Bauchant are well known in America, Vivin and Séraphine less so, and Eve, Rimbert and Peyronnet scarcely at all. Also unfamiliar to Americans is the Swiss, Adolf Dietrich, who has been greatly admired in Germany for almost twenty years.

Many of the American popular artists have already been exhibited in New York. Edward Hicks, probably the most important 19th century folk painter, and Joseph Pickett were shown in the exhibition of American Folk Art which Mr. Holger Cahill organized for the Museum of Modern Art in 1932. John Kane was included in the Museum's exhibition of Painting and Sculpture by Living Americans in 1930, several years before his death and posthumous fame. The paintings of Canadé, Branchard and Lebduska have often been seen in New York exhibitions; Hoyer, already widely appreciated in Chicago, and Pedro Cervantez have been shown in Federal Art Project exhibitions. Patrick J. Sullivan and Horace Pippin, the "discoveries" of Mr. Sidney Janis and Dr. Christian Brinton, respectively, should, however, prove something of a surprise to the public interested in art.

Canada is represented by the work of the blacksmith, Robert Cauchon, and the lumbermill hand, Chester Dalson.

A thorough combing of the field of popular art in America would probably reveal that several artists worthy of consideration have been omitted. It is hoped that this exhibition may lead to the discovery or revaluation of their work.

The European section of an exhibition of "modern primitives" was originally outlined three years ago by the Museum with the help of M. Wilhelm Uhde and Madame Jeanne Bucher, but it had to be twice postponed. In the meantime the energetic and alert director of the Grenoble Museum, M. Andry-Farcy, organized along similar lines the exhibition, *Les Maîtres Populaires de la Réalité*, which met with brilliant success in Paris during the summer of 1937 and has since been shown with alterations in Zurich and in London.

M. Andry-Farcy kindly consented to reserve many of the pictures in the Paris exhibition so that they could be included in the present show. In organizing the European section M. Andry-Farcy has been ably assisted by M. Henri Bing and M. Maximilien Gauthier;

Madame Gregory, Madame Bucher, and others have also coöperated most generously. The Museum wishes to extend its most cordial thanks to M. Andry-Farcy and those who have assisted him.

Mr. Holger Cahill, Director of the Federal Art Project, has generously assisted Miss Dorothy Miller of the Museum Staff in assembling the American Section. The French texts have been translated by Mrs. Frances Collins of the Museum staff.

The Museum of Modern Art wishes to thank the following for their help in assembling the exhibition and in preparing the catalog: Mr. Harry Wehle of the Metropolitan Museum of Art; Dr. Christian Brinton; Miss Florence Arquin, Mr. R. Vernon Hunter and Mr. Thomas C. Parker of the Federal Art Project; Mr. Max Weber; Mr. Sidney Janis; Mr. Valentine Dudensing; Mr. Stephan Bourgeois; Miss Marian Willard; Mrs. Margaret Gise; Miss Emily A. Francis; Mr. Carl Zigrosser; Mr. Fred Biesel; Mrs. Eula McClary; Viola Irene Cooper; Mr. James Johnson Sweeney; Miss Margaret Scolari; Dr. André Cournand; Dr. Walter Abell; Mr. Patrick Morgan; Mr. Robert W. Abendroth; Mr. and Mrs. Stanley Lee.

ALFRED H. BARR, JR.

# *The European Artists*

60 ROUSSEAU *Basket of Flowers*

# *Preface*

THE PAINTERS who concern us in this exhibition were innocent of the world. They did not know that when they began to paint they joined the brotherhood of Giotto and Delacroix, Tintoretto and Cézanne. They never lived like artists; they rarely thought or spoke in terms of art. Because their impulse to paint was of an absolute and unqualified purity, the feeling and taste which their work expresses are, undistorted, the feeling and taste of the class to which they belonged. They have a right to be called "artists of the people." They could find neither their themes nor their means of expression in the problems engaging other artists (many of whom erect so dense a screen between society and artistic expression that the "marxian" analysis of works of art has to be carried on with incredible subtlety and refinement). Instead they translated literally the dreams and thoughts of traditional France, a nation of artisans, half-peasant, half-bourgeois, a nation which produces great-hearted and simple men, lovers of flowers, painters and sculptors humorous and diligent.

The most anonymous, the most ingenuous and whimsical creations of the Middle Ages are now attributed to artists of this same stock. I say "attributed" in order to be cautious. It is always dangerous to speak of the genius of the common people and to claim to recognize its stamp in some song of unknown authorship, some pious or bantering piece of sculpture, some amusing decorative detail. But, on the other hand, it is impossible not to speak of this genius because, whether or not it is precisely defined, it is something we feel. The French are an ancient people; the Americans are still young; but we all know that this quality of soul exists and makes itself felt. And it is fortunate that we can find in contemporary art evidence of its survival and its permanence, in the face of social change, the succession of dominating classes and the formal order imposed by the development of esthetic problems. Despite the complicated machinery of these forces, the common people have preserved their integrity, their fecundity and their genuineness: taking their pleasure near at hand, taking their inspiration from sources other than the need to solve the problems of a theoretical universe. They find their inspiration in the actual universe, in all that lies about them, in reality and nature—though nature and reality do not necessarily mean to these artists, as one might assume, the "motif," the landscape seen through narrowed eyes: they may just as often mean a post-card. Post-cards were among the stimulants these men used when their imaginations flagged, the wine in which they found truth: very much as other artists found, and find, truth in museums. . . .

Thanks to our modest friends, a presence has again made its appearance in the history of art: the spirit of the people and of reality. The art of the middle ages teaches us that this presence has always made itself felt. And, looking carefully, we can find it among the great princes of art: the spirit of the people exists in Rembrandt and in Goya and in certain rough and lusty passages of Courbet, which conjure up the image of a tavern, or evoke the rude warmth of village life and make us realize that he, too, might well be considered an artist of the people. But never before our own period of wildly audacious intellectual speculation has the people's vision of reality been so purely stated by personalities so strong. Bombois, Vivin, Bauchant, Peyronnet: they show us how the act of painting can be as simple as breathing. Astonishing and inexhaustible revelation. These pictures were not painted for the ignorant: they were painted for the wise. Sunday painters? They are painters of all week, of every week, of eternity.

JEAN CASSOU
*Conservateur-Adjoint du Musée du Luxembourg*

# *Maîtres Populaires de la Réalité*

THOSE WHOM WE CALL *Maîtres Populaires de la Réalité*[1] are artists who, in our own time, have remained miraculously in a state of innocence. Theirs is the ingenuous habit of tackling the problem of expressing themselves through forms and colors borrowed from the world they see as though no one had ever struggled with that problem before them. They have not discovered the easy dodge of resorting to conventional attitudes, fashions and fixed opinions in the face of enigmas which the cultivated adult never wants to think about on the strange pretext that he is no longer a child. We do not wish to discount the importance, the elegance, the occasional courage of such cultivated attitudes, fashions and opinions: to do so would be to deny at one stroke the value of all training and all knowledge. But we must not forget their essential insecurity and the fact that in the end they are nothing but attitudes, fashions and opinions. The acts of the will, the precise gambits of the intelligence are to be respected. But the living truth is often more clearly seen in adage, catch-word and proverb than in dogma, postulate and thesis. Without the wisdom of the people, without *common* sense, there would be no Philosophy and no Art. But without Philosophy there would still be the wisdom of the people and, in consequence, there would still be Art.

Once this is clear, we can go on to say that the Maîtres Populaires de la Réalité may be loved and admired beyond all other artists without this love and admiration necessarily being restricted to them.

### *The Independence and True Traditionalism of the Popular Masters*

Strictly speaking, the Maîtres Populaires de la Réalité do not constitute a school. The painters whose work is grouped together here

[1]Literally translated: "popular masters of reality." The phrase is kept in the original French throughout M. Gauthier's article because it loses its precise flavor when translated. It is analyzed at the end of the article. *Editor.*

did not belong to the same generation. More than that; they either did not know one another or else they misunderstood one another. Unlike the Landscape Painters and the Romantics of 1830, the Realists of 1860, the Impressionists of 1890, the *Fauves* and Cubists of 1910, they were not united either by age or ideas, common friends or enemies, likes or dislikes. Their appearance as a group in exhibitions, or in the chapter which M. René Huyghe devotes to them in his history of modern art,[1] is not in the least their own doing. It is the work of those connoisseurs and critics who were the first to discover that a certain kinship existed among otherwise isolated artists. For Bombois is interested only in himself, and I can be very sure that if Vivin knew the paintings of Henri Rousseau, through the reproductions in M. Uhde's book on the *douanier*, he did not like them. These painters speak only for themselves but, through themselves, they speak for a creative tradition whose works reveal, across all boundaries of time and space, an identity which testifies to the existence of something permanent and continuous in the history of man's spirit and his works.

Knowing their lives, their backgrounds, their often rudimentary education and the perfect innocence of their hearts, we can declare with assurance that it is not because of any archaeological knowledge on their part that we recognize in their masterpieces elements which we — estheticians, connoisseurs, archaeologists — have already admired in rock paintings, archaic Greek and Asiatic sculpture, miniatures and frescoes of the middle ages, Romanesque capitals—all the masterpieces of so-called primitive art and so-called popular art. Without ever having thought of themselves as constituting a School, they have good grounds for assuming the name of a very ancient tradition, and they can do more than assume its name. Unconsciously, they

[1] *Cf. Histoire de l'Art Contemporain: La Peinture*, edited by René Huyghe, Paris, 1935. Chapter VII, *La Peinture d'Instinct*, contains an *Introduction* by René Huyghe and a section, *Henri Rousseau et les primitifs modernes*, by Wilhelm Uhde, who lists the following as important artists: Séraphine, Vivin, Bombois, Bauchant, Eve, Boyer and Rimbert. *Editor.*

are penetrated by this tradition, and they can no more paint except in obedience to it than they can live without breathing.

*The Discovery of Popular Art*

But—someone may say—if artists of this breed have always existed, how is it that we only now perceive their extraordinary importance?

In the first place, in the field of art—as in everything else—public opinion can long remain blind to the clearest evidence. African negro art and the art of the Pacific Islands did not begin yesterday: but they were overlooked almost as completely and as long as popular art. Then, too, many of the artists who came from the people confined their gifts almost entirely to the production of useful or modestly decorative objects. Richard Wagner said that the people alone create art: the artist can only seize upon and express the people's unconscious creation. In the archaeological museum of some small town, standing before a humble weather-vane, a ridge-pole ornament, the embellished diploma of some gymnastics teacher, a wrought-iron grille or a sign-board, we have felt the impact of fine art. And we have murmured that the men who made these things deserve oblivion far less than many who enjoy excessive fame. The magnificent artisans of our cathedrals, like the other honest workmen whose lives they shared, left few signatures behind them. Yet today, after centuries of indifference and contempt, these men are considered the founders of the most genuinely French art.

The people have always produced art spontaneously. Yet it was not until the middle of the last century that their art began to receive serious attention—thanks to the first romantics, the discoverers of the middle ages, who fought against italianate academicism for a national tradition. In the same period, history, clarified by Michelet who was himself a man of the people, ceased to concentrate on the great to the complete exclusion of the lowly. Although J. B. Thier's *Essay on Superstition* had revealed in 1679 a point of view comparable to that of Frazer and Sébillot, the word folk-lore did not come into use again until 1846. The science of folk-traditions, customs, beliefs, legends, art and literature must be counted among the contributions of the admirable 19th century. Only those unaware of this new field of knowledge could have considered it a poet's whim when in the early 20th century Guillaume Apollinaire heralded the *douanier* Rousseau, the greatest of the popular artists.

In 1848 the first open Salon was held, without a jury of admission. Only after 1885, however, the year in which the Salon des Indépendants was founded, did the popular artists annually have exhibition space at their disposal. Through these exhibitions connoisseurs, critics and the public came to discover that good painters existed outside the purlieus not only of officialdom but also of its revolutionary opponents. And because these exhibitions took place annually they also revealed that the popular artists were not merely able to bring off an occasional piece of fine work, perhaps by a stroke of luck, but that they were real masters, capable, like all real masters, of producing a *series* of works which were technically admirable and consistently related to one another.

Certain collectors have also played their part in bringing about this recognition. In Mme. Cécile Gregory's large studio overlooking the Seine the Maîtres Populaires de la Réalité were first assembled as a homogeneous group. I myself was already familiar with most of the painters, but in that studio I first had a chance to develop my theory of their basic kinship. I must also mention among the early champions of these artists, in France and abroad, Wilhelm Uhde, Marcel Monteux, Henri Bing, André Paz, François Meyer, Kurt Feldhaüser, Erick Charell, Dr. Franz Secker, Professor A. E. Brinckmann and Dr. Richard Moering.

### *"Popular" Art and "Modern" Art*

The recognition of the value of popular art has naturally had important esthetic implications. At the beginning of this century, after a hundred years of magnificent vitality comparable to the most fruitful periods of Greece, Italy and Holland; after David, Géricault, Delacroix, Ingres, Corot, Courbet, Manet, Cézanne, Seurat, Matisse and Bonnard, the French School was threatened by serious dangers. Art was on the verge of becoming a sort of super-algebra, no longer revealing reality, but revealing instead the artists' increasingly passionate search for plastic ingenuity, continuous revolution, innovation at any price. Before all else, before having anything to do with man, with flesh and blood and thought, a picture had to be a flat surface covered with colors arranged in a certain order. In every period and in every country artists had striven to make the abstract particular and concrete. Now, instead, it was a question of achieving the ultimate abstraction of the particular.

The Cubists and their friends, however, were the first[1] to be taken with the Maîtres Populaires de la Réalité: especially with Henri Rousseau. They wanted their pictures to contain something other than the official recipes for academic beauty and something other than Impressionism. The Impressionists had consecrated art to the rendering of delicate sensations. The Cubists wished to reintegrate in art human feeling and human thought. And they recognized that this was what Rousseau had done, in his own way, making more use of heart and impulse than of mind and will, attaining "naïvely" the objective toward which they were reaching intellectually.

At present when we see that most young artists are no longer concerned with abstract design but fight instead for a return to subject matter, the human element, the eternal verities, it looks as though the Maîtres Populaires de la Réalité have, in the end, won the day. But this development has been inevitable, in no way forced. The poetry which lies closest to the soul has always needed to use forms from the visible word in order to express itself in painting. We see this in Rembrandt. Jaurès said, justly, that reality is whatever is intelli-

[1]As M. Gauthier himself points out in his biographical note on Rousseau, page 41, Alfred Jarry and Rémy de Gourmont, during the early 1890's, were probably the first to take an interest in Rousseau. *Editor.*

gible. In order to become intelligible, in other words, in order to become communicable, a dream must clothe itself in the appearance of reality. These are the simple, the "naïve" truths which serve as remedies in the most severe crises of the intelligence. And the Cubists knew it, felt it, or suspected it. They could hurl themselves recklessly into a frenzy of experiment: the work of Rousseau, Vivin, Bombois and the others would still be there to demonstrate the efficacy of proven antidotes.

*The Problem of a Name*

For more than a quarter of a century popular masters have been known by all sorts of names: some highly suitable, some inappropriate.

Like so many of the major artists of the Renaissance, like Caravaggio, who was a plasterer's helper, most of these painters, in order to make a living, had to begin by working at jobs which, most of the time, had nothing to do with their vocation. But this did not make them mere "Sunday painters."[1]

It would be unfair to condemn all the artists whose financial circumstances or whose talent for getting along in the world of pedagogy or society has made it possible for them to paint every day in the week. It would be just as stupid to deny that a man who earns his living in some ordinary way can be a great artist. Once the problem has been solved of providing daily bread for himself and his family—the minimum of daily bread—such a man finds that he has won freedom more real and more complete than that of many "professionals" enslaved by routine.

[1]Louis Chéronnet has written: "People who love legends and anecdotes, who believe in the picturesque, will remember better than anything else that Henri Rousseau was a tax-collector, that Louis Vivin was a postal clerk, that Camille Bombois was a wrestler some of the time and a ditch-digger some of the time, that Dominique-Paul Peyronnet worked in a sugar-refinery and for a lithographer, that André Bauchant is a gardener and René Rimbert a chief postal clerk. Has all this any more essential importance than knowing that such and such a novelist is a government employee and that another has an inherited income? *What is important is that each of these artists saw only one thing: that he was before all else a painter, that is, a man compelled to give actual form to his vision of the world.*

Because of their direct and whole-hearted sincerity these painters are sometimes called "Naïves." The name is legitimate if the people who use it mean thereby to make them one with the heroes and the saints and all those whom Faith raises above the miserable level of our daily malice. They are naïve enough to be poets, to bestow their intimacy upon strangers. They are naïve if calling them naïve is meant to indicate that they are to be envied and admired. But why do people who consider themselves knowledgeable speak the word naïve with an air of superiority?

Still others have called these artists "Instinctives" and "Modern Primitives." They are not altogether wrong. To be unaware of the fact that it is possible to make use of methods devised by others in order to express one's own feeling and, despite this lack of awareness, to produce work which instantly bears the stamp of the masterpiece is to demonstrate the existence of a very powerful instinct: in other words, the existence of genius. And to paint without the slightest attention to the intellectual conventions which have dominated art since the Renaissance is to pass beyond the artificers, whom Montaigne denounced, to rejoin Giotto, Piero della Francesca and the Master of Villeneuve[1] and to carry on their work.

We still think it best to call them Maîtres Populaires de la Réalité.

"Popular"—to recall their folk origin, the magnificent simplicity of feeling and thought which is in their pictures and which is so like the feeling and thought we love in folk-songs and folk-tales. "Popular"—to make it very clear that their "atmosphere" has in it none of the unrest of so-called "modern" art.

"Masters" — and this is what really distinguishes them from so many other popular artists who exhibited at the Salon des Indépendants—by virtue of their real mastery of their profession, the sureness of their technique, the accomplished, original, distinctive character

[1]The painter of the Avignon or Villeneuve *Pietà*, often considered the greatest French painting of the XVth century. *Editor.*

of their way of composing and painting. Actually, on the score of painting nothing could be less naïve than a Rousseau or a Bombois. Nothing could be more concrete, decisive, lucid, more completely aware, more expert.

And Maîtres Populaires de la Réalité because—as Anatole France makes Sylvestre Bonnard say—the Universe is only a reflection of our soul. Vivin's dream is his reality. Bombois' realism is a dream of a world more luminous, sharper and stronger than the world we ordinarily see. And Rousseau's America has no more to do with geography than has Chateaubriand's. The Universe is only a reflection. True reality exists within the soul. And the reality which exists in certain simple and miraculous souls is Poetry. That is the whole secret.

MAXIMILIEN GAUTHIER

# *André Bauchant*

In 1922 André Bauchant wrote a letter to Maurice Raynal. In it he drew the following portrait of himself:

"André Bauchant was born at Châteaurenault on April 24, 1873. He went through the primary grades, and, having shown a certain aptitude in school, he was allowed to continue with his education till the age of fourteen. Then he was sent to work as a field-hand. Only after his military service was he able to resume his studies and his reading of the classics.

"For a month every year he traveled on business through central and western France. When he had time, when the day's work was done, he delighted in seeing local sights and antiquities. The taste for beauty was so alive in him that he still remembers a great deal of what he saw at that time.

"Reading about these ruins in French and foreign history books, I became increasingly attached to them: they truly seemed to tell the story of their ancient glories.

"As for museums, I visited them only as a layman, for I had no ideas about art and I could not estimate its value.

"During my youth I had such a real love for geography that I would hunt on maps for the smallest and most remote places. But it was only in 1917 that, on a friend's advice, I took a course in telemetry. This gave me a start. There were forty applicants for six places and the sketch I submitted at the examination won me first place. From then on I was given many opportunities, and as I was quick at the work I had plenty of time to learn.

"First I worked as an accountant behind the lines. In 1918, I was sent to Rheims as a draughtsman. Near Rheims I made the sketches of Marne landscapes which were exhibited in the Salon d'Automne in 1921.

"Of the pictures I have painted, these are my favorites: *Pericles justifying his Use of Public Funds* (*429 B.C.*), *The Assumption*,

BAUCHANT *Self-Portrait*

*The Battle of Thermopylae (July, 480 B.C.), Proclamation of American Independence (July 4, 1776)* (plate 3) and *Washington reading the Proclamation to his Troops before Rochambeau and LaFayette.*

"Since my first exhibition in 1921, thanks to which I was made a member of the Salon d'Automne, I have worked with increasing perseverance. This year I sent a selection of pictures to the National Society of Fine Arts. *The Battle of Palermo* (plate 1) and *The Expulsion of Adam and Eve* were accepted. I also painted *Perseus Rescuing Andromeda, The Dream of the Virgins, Almsgiving at the Door of the Village Church, Hippocrene, Pindus, Parnassus.*"

Since 1927, when he did the settings and costumes for a Stravinsky ballet which was produced in Monte Carlo by Diaghileff, Bauchant has given up painting large compositions of mythological and historical subjects and has concentrated chiefly on landscapes, figures and flowers. Though his work has often been exhibited, especially abroad, Bauchant has been wise enough to stay in the country. At present he lives in Touraine and when he is not painting he works in the fields and in his garden.

The Greeks and Romans in Bauchant's pictures are no more real than those of Nicolas Poussin, Louis David or Thomas Couture. But they are no less real either. Even when his imagination evokes the most heroic battles, it remains the imagination of a very simple man whose fantasy is unfettered by archaeological information. We do not expect of a picture what we would demand of a paper prepared for The Academy of Inscriptions and Belles-Lettres. Most of Bauchant's paintings delight us for reasons which are primarily pictorial—for their harmony of composition and color, for the liveliness and freedom of their drawing.

Bauchant speaks to us about history in a very intimate and gentle tone. His simple landscapes, his charming flowers shine in the light of the spirit of St. Francis and we can imagine him in his Touraine garden delivering a sermon to the birds.

M. G.

*1 THE BATTLE OF CARTHAGE (*or* THE BATTLE OF PALERMO). 1925
Oil on canvas, 37¾ x 57½ inches
Lent by Mme. Jeanne Bucher, Paris

*2 GREEK CHORUS. 1926
Oil on canvas, 39½ x 79 inches
Lent by Mme. Jeanne Bucher, Paris

*3 PROCLAMATION OF AMERICAN INDEPENDENCE. 1926
Oil on canvas, 28¾ x 45¾ inches
Lent by Mme. Jeanne Bucher, Paris

*4 FLOWERS IN PINK JUG. 1928
Oil on canvas, 40 x 28¾ inches
Lent by T. Catesby Jones, New York

5 FLOWERS. 1928
Oil on canvas
Lent anonymously

6 BEGONIAS. 1931
Oil on canvas, 57 x 41 inches
Lent by Dr. and Mrs. André Cournand, New York

7 MERCURY STEALING THE OXEN OF THE SUN. 1933
Oil on canvas, 23½ x 28¾ inches
Lent by Mme. Jeanne Bucher, Paris

*8 SHIPWRECK. 1933
Oil on canvas, 32 x 51¼ inches
Lent by Mme. Jeanne Bucher, Paris

9 THE TREACHERY OF JUDAS. 1933
Oil on canvas, 35 x 45¾ inches
Lent by Mme. Jeanne Bucher, Paris

*A star (*) before a catalog number indicates that the painting is illustrated by a plate which bears the same number.*
*The names of several European lenders were not received in time for inclusion in the catalog.*
*The sizes of paintings from European lenders have not been checked by the Museum staff.*

# *Camille Bombois*

Camille Bombois, the son of a river boatman, was born in 1883 at Venarey-les-Laumes, on the Côte d'Or. The first years of his life were spent on a barge. As I write these lines I can see Camille Bombois shrugging his great shoulders and grumbling in his thick dialect "Now you're starting that stuff about my being a ditch-digger." Bombois does not in the least want to deny his humble origin but he cannot stand being referred to as an eccentric, a workman who just happens to paint every once in a while. Painting is his only complete and compelling vocation. He has done other things, because he has had to earn his living and because he has occasionally yielded to the lure of adventure, but he has never followed any other calling. Yet since his painting is in essence the expression of all that he has experienced, it is relevant to mention that this superb interpreter of the poetry of waters was the son of a boatman and spent his early life on a barge.

When his father went to work for the Paris-Lyon-Méditerranée Railroad, Camille Bombois was sent to school. He felt quite restless there, prey to a nostalgia which was never to leave him. At the age of twelve he went to work on a farm at Migennes, near Laroche: he watched the cattle, he labored in the fields. At sixteen he began to sketch the life around him. He was very robust, muscular and pugnacious; he used to scuffle with his friends in the village square and soon he became the champion wrestler of the region. His greatest joy was to vanquish the strong-men in travelling circuses.

Eventually he joined Lucien Gay's circus. For many years he fought every day against professionals and amateurs. At twenty-three he left Lucien Gay for the Minard-Caron circus. The idea of Paris had been haunting him for a long time, but his travels took him only to the Upper Saône and the Upper Marne. To attain his wish he left the circus, turned laborer and step by step—always dreaming of canvases and paint brushes—he made his way to Paris where, in 1907, thousands of workmen were being recruited to build the subway.

At first Bombois worked near the Gare de l'Est. But his problem was by no means solved: he had to earn his living, provide for the needs of a household (he had married soon after arriving in Paris) and paint. It is not enough for an artist to have heart and mind filled with ideas and fervor. He needs light, and a man who has worked hard all day can scarcely paint at night—no matter how ardent his determination. But Bombois did not lose courage. He heard that strong men were needed to run newspaper presses. It was night work. He applied and was taken on. Then he replanned his life. He worked hard at night, slept six hours and painted the rest of the day. He was a painter, purely a painter—without the slightest wish to derive any material profit from the joy that painting gave him. For seven years Bombois lived in this way. They were fruitful years, during which he forged a technique, found his own style and produced as many pictures as some artists produce in a lifetime. To persist against such odds a man must have the love of painting in his blood and his heart must be full of faith.

In 1914 Bombois went to war; he was at the front for four and a half years and, because he is a man who never does things by halves, he won three decorations: the first at Chemin-Creux, the second at Chemin-des-Dames and the third during the night of the armistice—just to prove that he was not at all tired.

In 1922 Bombois ceased to paint exclusively for himself, his wife and a few friends. Not far from his lodging in the rue Coulaincourt some painters were getting ready an open air exhibition. Bombois decided to face what he calls "the judgment of the crowds." He placed his best picture on a chair and all around it on the ground he put a number of smaller canvases. Then he stood at a distance and watched, his heart quaking. Noel Bureau, the poet, was the first to become excited about the paintings. He bought one or two and wrote an article on Bombois in a little magazine of the period, called *Rythme et Synthèse.* Other admirers soon appeared, among them Florent Fels, Wilhelm Uhde, Madame Gregory, Mathot, Jacques Guenne and the writer. Bombois decided to spend all his time painting. Soon his pictures were being acquired by collectors.

Bombois' history explains his work. It is obviously the work of a powerful man. The forcefulness of his vision is athletic, and so is his masterful fashion of transferring it to canvas without hesitation or weakness. He disdains to make things easier for himself through the use of lighting effects. He sets his composition in the middle of a brilliant light which emphasizes the volume of the masses and the exquisite perfection of details. This is the secret of his lyricism. His purpose in using such lighting is to achieve a strictly accurate portrayal of the people and the things he knows.

At a recent Rousseau exhibition Bombois loyally admired the technique of the paintings but declared that they were not realistic enough for his taste. This is no place in which to make comparisons between the two artists. But we can say that in a picture by Bombois there is nothing which has not been inwardly experienced, solidly felt. He invents nothing, he distorts nothing on the pretext of artistic interpretation. He is neither an intellectual nor a priest, he is a man of the people, whose conception of the world derives from what he has learned through his muscles and his nerves. He cannot imagine an object except as it normally appears, nor can he conceive of a body or face conforming more than it actually does to theoretical canons of beauty. The figures he sets in his circus scenes and on the banks of his rivers make gestures and assume postures that are those of Bombois himself.

M. G.

10 THE CONVENT COURTYARD
Oil on canvas, 36¼ x 25½ inches

11 STILL LIFE WITH SPOTTED TABLECLOTH
Oil on canvas, 21¼ x 25½ inches

12 GYPSY ENCAMPMENT
Oil on canvas, 28¾ x 23½ inches

13 *FILLES*
Oil on canvas, 25½ x 36¼ inches
Collection F. M., Switzerland

*14 SACRE-COEUR. 1932
Oil on canvas, 39½ x 32 inches
Collection F. M., Switzerland

15 THE ARMANCON RIVER AND FACTORIES
Oil on canvas, 32 x 23½ inches

*16 GLEANERS
Oil on canvas, 23¾ x 28¾ inches

17 WASHERWOMEN
Oil on canvas, 18 x 25½ inches

18 CARD PLAYERS
Oil on canvas, 18 x 25½ inches

*19 CHARTRES
Oil on canvas, 28¾ x 23¾ inches
Lent by Mme. Cécile Gregory, Paris

20 CHURCH AT CHENY
Oil on canvas, 25½ x 32 inches
Lent by Mme. Cécile Gregory, Paris

*21 NUDE WITH ARMS RAISED
Oil on canvas, 32 x 25½ inches
Lent by Mme. Cécile Gregory, Paris

*22 GIRL READING IN A BOAT
Oil on canvas, 32 x 25½ inches

23 BRIDGE AT CHABLIS
Oil on canvas, 19¾ x 24 inches

*24 WOMEN WASHING CLOTHES
Oil on canvas, 28¾ x 36¼ inches
Lent by Mme. Cécile Gregory, Paris

25 THE WASTE LAND
Oil on canvas, 21¼ x 25½ inches

26 MUSCLES OF STEEL
Oil on canvas, 25½ x 32 inches

*27 THE FRIED-POTATO VENDOR
Oil on canvas, 18 x 25½ inches

*28 BEFORE ENTERING THE RING
Oil on canvas, 23¾ x 28¾ inches
Lent by Mme. E. Hostettler

*29 SELF PORTRAIT
Oil on canvas, 25½ x 21¼ inches
Lent by the Grenoble Museum

## *Adolf Dietrich*

Born at Berlingen, on the Swiss side of Lake Constance, November 19, 1877, Adolf Dietrich still lives in his native village. He owns a small house and garden, an acre of land, some fruit trees and a small vineyard. He raises rabbits and collects butterflies.

Dietrich's father wanted him to be a factory worker, a townsman. He spent fourteen years in a factory and then returned to his village and became a parish woodsman. He still practices this trade. He loves it almost as much as painting, and would continue with it even if he were offered a less humble position which would take him away from his beloved trees, his animals and his flowers.

He has always drawn. He was twenty-six when the painter Völmy came from Basle to paint at Berlingen. Dietrich watched him with wonder, and decided to take up painting. That is his whole story. In 1916, in a book called *Le Livre de Bodensée*, he published some drawings which were noticed by the director of the Museum of Art at Baden. The Museum exhibited them. Later, Mr. Herbert Tannenbaum of Mannheim became interested in Dietrich and was responsible for the acquisition of his work by German museums and many Swiss, German and French private collections.

Dietrich's simple art, precise and energetic, exhales a strong perfume of rustic poetry. It consists of landscapes, figure pieces, still-lifes, flower pictures and portraits of animals.

*30 MAN WITH A PIPE. 1926
Oil on cardboard, 20 x 12⅞ inches

*31 FOXES IN THE FOREST. 1923
Oil on cardboard, 18⅜ x 22 inches

32 YOUNG GIRL IN RED SWEATER. 1936
Oil on wood, 17¾ x 11½ inches

33 OLD MAN. 1930
Oil on cardboard, 24¼ x 20 inches

34 LAKE CONSTANCE. 1931
Oil on canvas, 18 x 33⅝ inches

35 A WARM WIND. 1931
Oil on cardboard, 19 x 20¾ inches

*36 MORNING ON THE LAKE. 1934
Oil on wood, 23½ x 18½ inches

37 THE LETTER. 1936
Oil on wood, 7½ x 7½ inches

# *Jean Eve*

Born in 1900, at Somain in the north of France, Jean Eve's first attempts at painting date from his fifteenth year. "No one," he says, "ever taught me anything." He painted, so he thought, for distraction, to escape through an amusing game the difficulties of an apprentice's life. He had no intention of becoming an artist.

Eve did his military service in Syria, but nothing in his work indicates that he remembers it. (At the time he was interested in watercolors and amused himself with a sort of elementary dot-technique.) On his return to France he found employment as an industrial draughtsman, then as book-keeper in a foundry and finally as a mechanic in an automobile factory near Paris. In 1924 he saw the Courbet exhibition in Paris. "It hit me so hard," he says, "that it awoke in me a need to paint in earnest, to remake what I saw."

In 1928 Eve made the acquaintance of Kisling, to whom he had been drawn by a book of Jacques Guenne's. From that time on people began to take notice of him and exhibitions of his work were held. At one point he even left the factory and settled down to paint in the neighborhood of Mantes. But he soon turned homeward and went back to earning a living: he has a wife and children to support, and he would be reluctant to paint unless he had the assurance of being able to provide for them. In 1935, through a competitive examination, Eve succeeded in getting a night-job in the Paris toll-house. This guarantees his livelihood and leaves the day free for his art.

M. G.

*38 BOULEVARD SAINT-DENIS AT COURBEVOIE. 1937
Oil on canvas, 21¼ x 28¾ inches

39 TOWN OF MARCON-SUR-LOIRE. 1937
Oil on canvas, 18 x 25½ inches

*40 GYPSY ENCAMPMENT. 1937
Oil on canvas, 18⅛ x 25⅝ inches
Lent by Maximilien Gauthier, Paris

41 AUTUMN LANDSCAPE
Oil on canvas, 18 x 25½ inches

42 WINTER SOLITUDE. 1935
Oil on canvas, 13 x 18 inches

# *Dominique-Paul Peyronnet*

Dominique-Paul Peyronnet was born at Talence, near Bordeaux, in September, 1872. Until his retirement in 1920 he was a very successful printer, specializing in color lithography.

After his military service Peyronnet worked at Bayonne, Angoulême, Cognac, Montpelier, Roubaix, Amiens, Saumur, Rennes and Alençon. In 1902 he arrived in Paris, and for eighteen years he worked in a printing shop on the rue Suger from whose presses came thousands of the brilliantly colored school-book covers which have brightened the lives of several generations of Parisian children. Peyronnet loved his trade and earned his living easily. Every summer he and Mme. Peyronnet spent several days at Villers-sur-Mer, near Tréport, lunching and dining on the cliffs beside the sea. From the cliffs Peyronnet watched the waves, estimating how many colors he would need to combine on the stone in order to express their infinite changes.

From 1914 to 1918 Peyronnet fought in the war. In 1915 he was gassed. After leaving the hospital he was set to distributing stores and ammunition, assigned to the telephone service and, finally, removed from the scene of action and sent to Italy to learn how to print from zinc. They were dark years, separated from all that he loved. About 1920 Peyronnet decided to devote himself exclusively to painting. He began with small woodland scenes, which were agreeably impressionistic, but he wearied soon of such banalities, found his own language and confirmed his style. In 1932 he exhibited at the Indépendants and at the Salon de l'Ecole Française. From then until 1935 he exhibited regularly only at the Indépendants, where, in 1934, he showed *The Castle of the White Queen* and *The Divan.* There were several of us who acquired the habit of looking for Peyronnet's pictures at the Indépendants every year, but the first connoisseur to buy several of his canvases was Mme. Cécile Gregory.

In 1936 Peyronnet was represented in the competition for the Paul Guillaume prize by *The Ferryman of the Moselle*, now in the Gregory Collection. (Plate 43.) No one denies the dramatic strength of this painting. The subject was suggested by a street song based on an episode in the war of 1870: the ferry-man of the Moselle, commanded to transport a German troop across the river, cuts the cable and dies with the enemy rather than betray France.

When *The Ferryman of the Moselle* was shown in the Paul Guillaume exhibition, Peyronnet heard an obviously incompetent visitor say that he was probably imitating Rousseau. Anxious to discover if this was so, Peyronnet rushed to the Louvre. He returned distressed. He had looked at the paintings of Theodore Rousseau and he could not see how his work resembled them.

Peyronnet imitates no one. With patience, with taste and with the care of a master artisan, he covers his canvas with thousands of little brush strokes. In his simplicity, he believes that he is reproducing with perfect accuracy the world he sees. He does not realize that he is, instead, establishing order and equilibrium in his own soul.

M. G.

*43 THE FERRYMAN OF THE MOSELLE
Oil on canvas, 35 x 45¾ inches
Lent by Mme. Cécile Gregory, Paris

*44 FOREST LANDSCAPE
Oil on canvas, 23½ x 32 inches

45 FOGGY SEA
Oil on canvas, 21¼ x 32 inches

46 VILLERS-SUR-MER
Oil on canvas, 25½ x 32 inches

*47 THE MODEL
Oil on canvas, 23¾ x 32 inches

*48 THE OPEN SEA
Oil on canvas, 21¼ x 32 inches
Collection F. M., Switzerland

49 CLIFFS AND THE SEA
Oil on canvas, 21¼ x 32 inches

*50 THE FIELDS OF CHARENTE
Oil on canvas, 25½ x 32 inches

# *René Rimbert*

Born in Paris in 1896, René Rimbert is now a chief postal clerk. His father was an artisan, a wood carver and, sometimes, a picture restorer. René Rimbert went to public school and later continued his education by taking free high-school courses at night and whenever his work left him time during the day. He entered the postal service at the age of seventeen and was twenty when his class was called to war. Rimbert served first in the artillery and later was transferred to Headquarters as a draughtsman. In 1919, soon after his marriage, he travelled in Belgium, Germany and Austria, and his visits to museums inspired in him a boundless admiration for Vermeer of Delft, whom he esteems above all other painters.

Since boyhood Rimbert has drawn and has been interested in music. As a child growing up in the 16th *arrondissement* he sang in the choir of Saint-Sulpice.

Gromaire was the first to notice Rimbert's work at the 1920 Salon des Indépendants, where he was exhibiting for the second time. Later both André Level and Max Jacob, the author of *Le Cornet à Dés*, became interested in him. "In his landscapes," writes Jacob, "there is something of the peace of nature: it looks as though he had sworn to rival the silence of the inanimate; his trees share the earth's tranquility; it is no longer Corot's paradise that we see: it is another, a terrestrial paradise. Rimbert never worries about the outcome of a picture; it is finished before it is begun; he is ready to paint; he approaches his canvas with a calm which draws us closer to God."

René Rimbert draws and paints with admirable precision, without blurring his outlines or sacrificing literal color to atmospheric effects. He likes calm compositions, wide, luminous skies, pure rhythms and delicate color harmonies. He is above all the painter of the Left Bank and of Saint-Sulpice, that quarter of Paris whose calm recalls the austere grace we sometimes find in Rome.

M. G.

51 VIEW OF THE RUE DE RENNES. 1924
Oil on canvas, 36¼ x 23½ inches
Collection G. P., Paris

52 COURTYARD ON SUNDAY MORNING. 1925
Oil on canvas, 25½ x 18 inches

*53 STREET SCENE WITH NUN. 1927
Oil on canvas, 25½ x 21¼ inches
Collection G. P., Paris

54 POT OF HYACINTHS. 1929
Oil on canvas, 25½ x 18 inches
Collection G. P., Paris

55 VIEW OF THE CITY. 1929
Oil on canvas, 39½ x 32 inches
Collection G. P., Paris

*56 SUNNY ROAD AT PERPEZAC-LE-NOIR. 1930
Oil on canvas, 28¾ x 19¾ inches
Collection G. P., Paris

57. RUE DU DRAGON. 1930
Oil on canvas, 32 x 25½ inches
Lent by the Grenoble Museum

*58 MORNING IN THE COURTYARD. 1924
Oil on canvas, 21¾ x 15 inches

# *Henri Rousseau*

Books and articles about Henri Rousseau abound in shafts of wit, touching anecdotes, tender and not always respectful recollections, and intrusions, sometimes in doubtful taste, into his private life. These alternate with learned discursions in the course of which the writer, caried away by the contemplation of his own nobility in defending and interpreting so extraordinary a genius, succeeds in hiding from us completely the painter, his work and the sort of man he actually was. We can only conclude, with Philippe Soupault, that the only really authentic biographical information about Rousseau is the information he himself has left us. This is included in a brief note that Rousseau wrote for Girard-Coutances who, in 1895, was preparing the second volume of his *Portraits of the Next Century*. Here it is:

HENRI ROUSSEAU

*Painter*

"Born at Laval, in 1844, because of his parents' poverty he was obliged to follow a career other than that to which he was impelled by his feeling for art.

"It was only in 1885, after long vexation, that he started to paint: all alone, with nature for his only teacher—and a little advice from Gérôme and Clément. He sent two pictures, the first of his work to be exhibited, to the Salon des Champs-Elysées. They were *Italian Dance* and *Sunset.*

"The next year he painted: *Carnival Evening; A Thunderclap; Waiting; A Poor Devil; After the Feast; Departure; Dinner on the Grass; The Suicide; Myself: for my Father*, a self-portrait and landscape; *Tiger Pursuing Explorers; Centenary of Independence; Liberty; The Last of the 41st;* and *The War*, a genre portrait of Alfred Jarry, the author; in addition he did about 200 drawings in

Henri Rousseau. From a photograph owned by Max Weber. Inscribed: *Offert à mon ami Weber artiste peintre. Paris, le 14/12, 1908. Henri Rousseau artiste peintre.*

pen and ink and pencil and a few landscapes of Paris and its environs.

"Only after grave trials did he succeed in making himself known to a few of the artists around him. He perfected himself in the unique field which he had made his own, and he is now on the way to becoming one of our best realistic painters.

"He may be identified by the fact that he wears a bushy beard and that he has been connected with the Indépendants for a long time. He believes that complete creative freedom should be left to the artist, whose thoughts soar into the realm of the beautiful and the good.

"He will never forget those journalists who really understood him, who kept him going during periods of discouragement and who helped him to become what he was destined to be.

"Paris, July 10, 1895."

On the other hand, we *do* know that Rousseau's father sold pots and pans and that his mother attended church regularly. Why should we not believe him when he says that their poverty was all that prevented his becoming a painter right away? Jean-Jacques Rousseau was a lawyer's clerk, an engraver's apprentice, a novice, a domestic servant, a music-teacher and a schoolmaster before he became a man of letters. Yet he has never been thought of as a "Sunday writer." Rousseau says not a word about serving as a musician with the army in Mexico. Was he ever really there? There are those who doubt it. At the beginning of that campaign Rousseau was eighteen and, according to Soupault, had already served three years with the army. Nor does Rousseau enlarge on the war of 1870, during which he was a sergeant: a rank which would have entitled him, after the Treaty of Frankfort, to just such a job in the toll-house as we know he had. Will all this be verified some day? In his youth he was madly in love with a Polish woman named Jadwiga, and her memory inspired one of his most famous pictures, *The Dream*. He married; his wife died; he remarried and was again widowed. He had a daughter, Julia, who lived in Angers after her marriage. On September 2, 1910, at the age of sixty-six, Henri Rousseau died in the Necker hospital of a chill he had caught standing at night under the window of a woman of fifty, a woman who spurned him because he was too poor, in spite of all his pictures and all the trouble he had gone to teaching singing, piano and violin in his modest studio at 2 *bis* rue Perrel, in Plaisance.

Pissarro and Gauguin knew Rousseau and valued his art highly. Gauguin considered his blacks incomparable. Alfred Jarry[1] and Rémy de Gourmont took an interest in him. But he received the

[1]J. J. Sweeney refers us to an article in *Les Soirées de Paris*, Paris, Jan. 15, 1916, by Guillaume Apollinaire, who writes: "It was incontestably M. Rémy de Gourmont who first encouraged the painter of Plaisance. He even commissioned Rousseau to do a lithograph, *Les Horreurs de la Guerre* which was published in *L'Imagier. . . .*" This occurred in 1893. Apollinaire states, however, that it was Jarry who discovered Rousseau. They were both from the same town, Laval. Mr. Sweeney gives other references which indicate that Serusier, Guérin, Toulouse-Lautrec, and Degas were among the artists of the '90s who knew Rousseau or his work. *Editor*.

most effective support from the Brummer brothers. They themselves were poor at that time, but they still did not hestitate to buy Rousseau's work with what little money they had; and they converted their friends. Joseph Brummer, who has since become one of New York's important art dealers, had his portrait painted by Rousseau, a picture which is now considered one of the *douanier's* most forceful works. Above all, we must mention Wilhelm Uhde, who knew Rousseau in 1907, devoted a monograph to him as early as 1911 and organized the famous retrospective exhibition[1] which was held in 1912. Among other friends and admirers who backed Rousseau during his life time were Picasso, Derain, Vlaminck, Robert Delaunay, Brancusi, and, among the writers, Guillaume Apollinaire, André Salmon, Max Jacob and Georges Duhamel.

Henri Rousseau painted landscapes, still lifes, portraits and large compositions. He was a real artist, and, as a painter, not in the least naïve. He was naïve only in the degree to which he gave himself up to the problem of painting the world and its creatures exactly as he saw them. His was a good and simple heart, and his soul was the pure soul of a man to whom poetry and nature are one and the same thing. Yet this was not the primary basis of his art. Such spirits are less rare than we are inclined to suppose, and Rousseau might have remained unknown or misunderstood, like so many others, had he not been a great painter. He was a painter without any weakness; each of his pictures is the extraordinary product of disciplined knowledge and awareness. Into everything he did he projected the full force of his will, his conviction, his desire for powerful expression and perfect precision. He always succeeded in realizing his intention plastically,

[1]An exhibition of Rousseau's work was held in New York two years before this at Alfred Stieglitz gallery at 291 Fifth Avenue. Max Weber, the American painter, introduced Rousseau to America. He had been Rousseau's devoted friend in Paris and had even sung tenor at some of Rousseau's musicales. He was instrumental in arranging the exhibition at "291" which opened, November, 1910, a month after Rousseau's death. The tiny still life (plate 71) in this exhibition was given to Mr. Weber by Rousseau with the touching dedication noted under its catalog entry. *Editor.*

without any recourse to convenient surface ingenuities. This dreamer was a capable workman, able to build his dream into a solid and marvelously balanced reality. This supposed ignoramus knew all that he needed to know about proportions, rhythms, colors and forms: those qualities which form the connecting link between classical masterpieces of every period and every country. He did not know what Giotto was all about. But *like* Giotto he knew how to subordinate anatomy (that "dreadful science" as Ingres himself called it) to the higher needs of expression, and through the very intensity with which he attacked the problem of literal representation he achieved at one and the same time the particular and the general, the actual and the symbolic.

M. G.

*59 LE CHÂTEAU FORT. 1889
Oil on canvas, 36½ x 28¾ inches
Lent by Mr. and Mrs. William Averell Harriman, New York

*60 BASKET OF FLOWERS
Oil on canvas, 15 x 18 inches
Lent by William S. Paley, New York
*Color plate preceding page 15.*

61 VASE OF FLOWERS. 1901-1902
Oil on canvas, 18¼ x 13 inches
Lent by William S. Paley, New York

*62 PORTRAIT OF A YOUNG GIRL
Oil on canvas, 24 x 18 inches
Lent by R. Sturgis Ingersoll, Penlynn, Pennsylvania

*63 JUNGLE
Oil on canvas, 45 x 64 inches
Lent by Miss Adelaide Milton de Groot, courtesy The Metropolitan Museum of Art, New York

*64 JUNGLE WITH LIONS
Oil on canvas, 14¾ x 17½ inches
Lent by The Adolph Lewisohn Collection, New York

65 JUNGLE WITH A LION
Oil on canvas, 14¾ x 18 inches
The Museum of Modern Art, The Lillie P. Bliss Collection

*66 JUNGLE WITH TWO MONKEYS. 1900-1910
Oil on canvas, 25 x 19 inches
Lent by Mrs. Charles S. Payson, New York

*Note:* This is said to be the painting which figured in the lawsuit of January, 1909, when Rousseau was accused of helping to swindle the Bank of France of 21,000 francs. He painted this canvas in order to impress the court with his artistic ability. He was convicted but his obvious innocence of any criminal intention and the fact that this was his first offence caused his light sentence to be suspended.

*67 THE UMBRELLA
Oil on canvas, 13 x 16 inches
Lent by Mrs. Charles S. Payson, New York

*68 THE PINK CANDLE
Oil on canvas, 6⅜ x 8¾ inches
Lent by the Phillips Memorial Gallery, Washington, D. C.

69 PALETTE. 1907
Oil on wood, 8⅞ x 6⅜ inches
Inscribed: *Henri. E.G. Mai 1907*
Lent by Mrs. John D. Rockefeller, Jr., New York

70 NOTRE-DAME. 1909
Oil on canvas, 13 x 16 inches
Lent by the Phillips Memorial Gallery, Washington, D. C.

*71 STILL LIFE
Oil on wood, 2⅞ x 5½ inches
Inscribed on stretcher: *Offert à mon ami Weber, le 20 d'août 1908, Union de l'Amérique et de la France, les 2 Républiques. Henri Rousseau.*
Lent by Max Weber, Great Neck

*72 ÎLE DE LA CITE
Oil on canvas, 6 x 9½ inches
Lent by Mrs. Rose Gershwin, New York

72A MOTHER AND CHILD
Oil on canvas, 8⅝ x 6½ inches

72B HOUSE NEAR PARIS
Oil on canvas, 13 x 18¼ inches

72C STREET SCENE
Oil on canvas, 10¼ x 13¾ inches

72D "PATACHE D'AVAL, QUAI D'AUTUIL"
Ink, 6⅜ x 4¾ inches

72E "QUAI D'AUTUIL"
Ink, 6⅛ x 4⅛ inches
Nos. 72A-E lent by Max Weber, Great Neck

# *Séraphine Louis*

Séraphine Louis, called Séraphine de Senlis, was born at Assy in the Oise district in 1864. In 1934 she died in a home for the aged.

One day in 1912, Wilhelm Uhde, who used to spend his summers in Senlis, called at the house of some humble neighbors. To their great amusement, he stopped short in admiration before a still life on their wall. They told him that the artist was Séraphine, his charwoman.

In her childhood Séraphine attended to the younger children in the family and took care of the livestock. She went to Senlis and there became a drudge, performing the meanest chores. She was very pious, even mystic: a votive light burned always before the image of the Virgin. The joys which existence denied her she found in a marvelous world of her own, and she learned to transfer this world to canvas, using translucent colors, like those in stained glass windows, which yet possessed the perfect quality of enamel. Sometimes she painted trees with shells instead of leaves, flowers with staring eyes, fruits like living animals, water as deep as infinity. There is not one picture of Séraphine's which was not painted, as M. Uhde has pertinently said, with rare passion, with sacred fervor and medieval ardor. That ardor, which became in her a compelling ecstasy, driving her to paint according to unknown laws, was the true ardor of the people. For the colors, the forms and the rhythms of Séraphine's pictures exist in the sculpture, the embroidery and the painting produced by the peasant artists of every century. M. G.

*73 CLUSTER OF FRUITS
Oil on canvas, 45⅝ x 35 inches

*74 AUTUMN LEAVES
Oil on canvas, 45¾ x 35 inches

75 BRIGHT FOLIAGE
Oil on canvas, 36¼ x 28¾ inches

76 PLANT
Oil on canvas, 36¼ x 28¾ inches

Nos. *74-76 lent by Wilhelm Uhde, Paris

77 DAISIES
Oil on canvas, 30 x 23½ inches

78 LILACS
Oil on canvas, 25½ x 32 inches

79 FRUITS
Oil on canvas, 36¼ x 28¾ inches
Lent by the Grenoble Museum

# *Louis Vivin*

Born in July, 1861, in Hadol, a small village near Epinal, Louis Vivin died in May, 1936, in the modest Montmartre lodging where he had lived for more than fifty years. During all that time Vivin and his wife were unable to consign to the dust-bin any object which had made its way into their home, and their rooms became a sentimental museum of lower middle-class life. I shall never forget their singular charm, any more than I shall forget Vivin himself, bearded like a patriarch, noble and debonair in the midst of his strange bazaar.

One day I noticed a reproduction of Millet's *Angelus* pasted on the wall of Vivin's house. I asked the old man if he admired Millet. "No," he answered mildly. I persisted. He thought for a long time, examined the picture closely and then presented his verdict: "Don't you find it a little vulgar?"

The phrase casts a light on Vivin himself, master of an art so spiritualized that it achieves results comparable to those sought by Surrealism.

The son of a school teacher, Vivin attended the Industrial School at Epinal. From his earliest youth he was passionately fond of drawing and even the doors of his family's house were covered with his scribblings. When the parish priest gave him a box of watercolors the child made up his mind to be a painter, but his father disapproved.

In 1881 (a year before his only child was born) Vivin went to work at the Central Post Office in Paris. He was in turn a letter carrier, a chief clerk, a department head and, finally, an inspector, the rank with which he retired at the age of sixty-two. A large map on which he had carefully marked all the post-offices in France earned him the congratulations of his superiors and an Academy award.

In spite of his father's opposition, Louis Vivin has always been an artist. We know of landscapes painted about 1880, probably from memory, views of his native countryside, whose sober color and tranquil style recall Far-Eastern art. Wilhelm Uhde assigns to the year 1890 (seven years before Rousseau painted his famous *Sleeping Gypsy*) a very large landscape of a swamp and a heron. But it was only after 1922 that Vivin could devote himself exclusively to painting. Then began the evolution from the dreamlike realism of his early pictures to the quasi-Surrealist character of his later work. It was a question of true creation. I can testify that Vivin knew none of the artists of his time, never set foot in an exhibition, never read a single piece of art criticism. Before he became well-known in 1932 at the Foire aux Croûtes in Montmartre, he sold his pictures to passers-by in the market place of Sacré-Coeur. He did this not because he needed money but because he wanted to share with as many people as possible the good that he had found, and because self-respect forbade his giving his work away.

Vivin's work varies greatly in subject matter. It includes pictures of Parisian life along the banks of the Seine and in the suburbs, scenes filled with people, the backgrounds often painted so abstractly that they are reduced to little more than sets against which the drama of human life is enacted. He also painted still lifes, interiors, hunt meetings and family gatherings. His early work is so adroitly realistic that one could never ascribe the manner characteristic of his later paintings to incompetence or awkwardness. Little by little, Vivin discovered that the only true reality is the reality of thought and feeling, and so we find him taking greater and greater liberties with material considerations, with the laws of perspective and of gravity. Into the crucible of his dream he threw the forms and colors of the common world, and drew forth a marvelous new world in which were blended the poet's spirit and the world we all know, purified and adorned with exquisite colors.

M. G.

80 ARRIVAL OF THE PEDDLERS
Oil on canvas, 18 x 24 inches
Collection F. M., Switzerland

81 SACRE-COEUR
Oil on canvas, 23½ x 28¾ inches

*82 STILL LIFE WITH OYSTERS
Oil on canvas, 21¼ x 25½ inches
Lent by Mme. Cécile Gregory, Paris

*83 QUAI DE L'HORLOGE
Oil on canvas, 28¾ x 39½ inches
Lent by Mme. Cécile Gregory, Paris

84 RHEIMS CATHEDRAL
Oil on canvas, 25½ x 19¾ inches
Lent by Mme. Cécile Gregory, Paris

*85 PLACE DU TERTRE IN WINTER. 1929
Oil on canvas, 19¾ x 24 inches
Lent by Mme. Cécile Gregory, Paris

86 NOTRE-DAME
Oil on canvas, 32 x 25½ inches
Collection F. M., Switzerland

*87 WILD BOAR CHASED BY DOGS
Oil on canvas, 23½ x 36¼ inches

88 DEER IN THE SNOW
Oil on canvas, 21¼ x 25½ inches

*89 CHURCH INTERIOR
Oil on canvas, 25½ x 21¼ inches
Lent by Wilhelm Uhde, Paris

90 THE TUILERIES
Oil on canvas, 13 x 18 inches

91 CHURCH OF ST. LAURENT AND THE GARE DE L'EST
Oil on canvas, 18 x 24 inches
The Museum of Modern Art, gift of Mrs. Sadie A. May

# *Short Bibliography*

This bibliography contains only the more important references to European popular painting. The reader will find indispensable for further study the biblographies on pp. 194-6 of the *Histoire de l'Art Contemporain: La Peinture* (Paris, Alcan, 1935), edited by René Huyghe.

## *General*


CASSOU, JEAN. "Les Maîtres Populaires de la Réalité," *Art Vivant*, Aug.-Sept., 1937, no.214, p.201-3.

GUENNE, JACQUES. "La Naïvété Est-Elle un Art?" *Art Vivant*, 1931, v.7, p.140.

HUYGHE, RENÉ. "La Peinture d'Instinct; Introduction." In: *Histoire de l'Art Contemporain: La Peinture. Publiée sous la direction de René Huyghe.* Paris, Alcan, 1935. p.185-8.

LHOTE, ANDRÉ. "Art Populaire," *Nouvelle Revue Française*, Aug. 1, 1929, v.16, p.274-6.

Musée de Grenoble à Paris. *Les Maîtres Populaires de la Réalité. Avant-propos de Raymond Escholier; textes et notices de Maximilien Gauthier.* 1937.
Exhibition catalog.

Tooth, Arthur, & Sons, Ltd., London. *Les Maîtres Populaires de la Réalité.* Feb.17-Mar.12, 1938.
Exhibition catalog: introduction and biographies in English.

UHDE, WILHELM. "Henri Rousseau et les Primitifs Modernes." In: *Histoire de l'Art Contemporain: La Peinture. Publiée sous la direction de René Huyghe.* Paris, Alcan, 1935. p.189-196.
Contains extensive biographical and bibliographical notes.

———. *Picasso and the French Tradition.* Paris, Editions des Quatre Chemins; New York, Weyhe, 1929. p.71-79.

———. *Von Bismarck bis Picasso; Erinnerungen und Bekentnisse.* Zurich, Verlag Oprecht, 1938. p.150-2, 156-8, 247-54.

## *Monographs on Individual Artists*


BAUCHANT, ANDRE

GEORGE, WALDEMAR. "Populism or Romanism: André Bauchant," *Formes*, Feb. 1931, no.12, p.25-6.

RAYNAL, MAURICE. *Modern French Painters*. New York, Brentano's, 1928. p.35-7.

*Les Simples Vus par Violette; douze planches en couleurs d'André Bauchant.* Paris, Bucher, 1937.

BOMBOIS, CAMILLE

BING, H. "The Limits of Popular Art," *Formes*, Feb., 1930, no.2, p.8-10.

DELTEIL, JOSEPH. "Bombois, Painter in Painting," *Formes*, Feb., 1930, no.2, p.7.

FRANK, NINO. "Bombois," *Art Vivant*, 1929, v.5, p.295.

DIETRICH, ADOLF

RIESS, MARGOT. "Der Maler Dietrich," *Kunst für Alle*, 1927, v.43, p.55-62. Also published in *Die Kunst*, 1927, v.29, p.55-62.

EVE, JEAN

FRANK, NINO. "Jean Ève," *Art Vivant*, 1930, v.6, p.618.

ROUSSEAU, HENRI

BASLER, ADOLPHE. *Henri Rousseau, Sa Vie—Son Oeuvre*. Paris, Librairie de France, 1927.

———. *Henri Rousseau*. Paris, Librairie de France, n.d. (Series: Les Albums d'Art Druet.)

———. *Henri Rousseau*. Paris, Nouvelle Revue Française, 1927. (Series: Peintres Nouveaux.)

*Dodici Opere di Rousseau*. Firenze, Libreria della Voce, 1914. (Series: Maestri Moderni.)

DZITTYA, EMIL. *Henri Rousseau.* Hamburg, Asmus Verlag, 1924.

Galerie Alfred Flechtheim, Berlin. *Ausstellung Henri Rousseau, 1926.* Berlin, Das Kunstarchiv Verlag, 1926.

GREY, ROCH. *Henri Rousseau.* Roma, Valori Plastici, 1922. (Series: Les Artistes Nouveaux.)
Second edition published in 1924.

*Henri Rousseau, le Douanier.* London, The Studio, 1936. (Series: The World's Masters.)

KOLLE, HELMUD. *Henri Rousseau.* Leipzig, Klinkhardt & Biermann, 1922. (Series: Junge Kunst.)

SALMON, ANDRÉ. *Henri Rousseau, Dit le Douanier.* Paris, Crès, 1927. (Series: Peintres et Sculpteurs.)

SOUPAULT, PHILIPPE. *Henri Rousseau, le Douanier.* Paris, Editions des Quatre Chemins, 1927.

UHDE, WILHELM. *Henri Rousseau.* Paris, Figuière, 1911.

———. *Henri Rousseau.* Dusseldorf, Galerie Alfred Flechtheim, 1914.

———. *Henri Rousseau. 2te Auflage.* Berlin, Kaemmerer, 1923.

ZERVOS, CHRISTIAN. *Henri Rousseau.* Paris, Cahiers d'Art, 1927. (Series: Les Grands Peintres d'Aujourd'hui.)

SÉRAPHINE LOUIS

UHDE, WILHELM. "Painters of the Inner Light: Séraphine," *Formes,* 1931, no. 17, p. 115-7.

VIVIN, LOUIS

UHDE, WILHELM. "The Meticulous Art of Louis Vivin," *International Studio,* Sept., 1930, v.97, p.28-32, 78.

B. N.

1 BAUCHANT *The Battle of Carthage* (or *The Battle of Palermo*). 1925

2 BAUCHANT *Greek Chorus.* 1926

3 BAUCHANT *Proclamation of American Independence*. 1926

4 BAUCHANT *Flowers in Pink Jug*. 1928

8 BAUCHANT *Shipwreck*. 1933

14 BOMBOIS *Sacré-Coeur*. 1932

16 BOMBOIS *Gleaners*

19 BOMBOIS *Chartres*

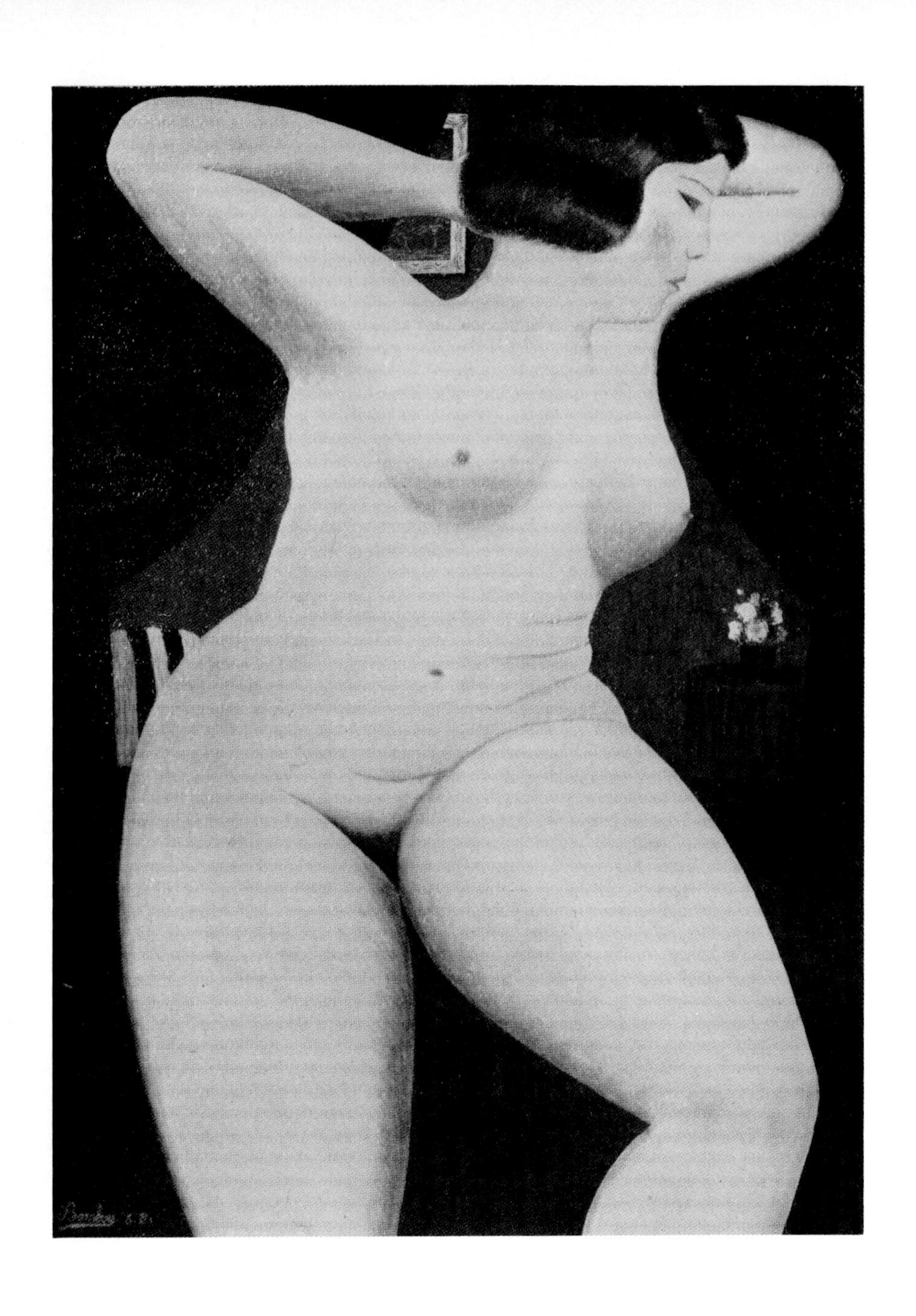

21 BOMBOIS *Nude with Arms Raised*

22 BOMBOIS *Girl Reading in a Boat*

24 BOMBOIS *Women Washing Clothes*

27 BOMBOIS *The Fried-Potato Vendor*

28 BOMBOIS *Before Entering the Ring*

29 BOMBOIS *Self Portrait*

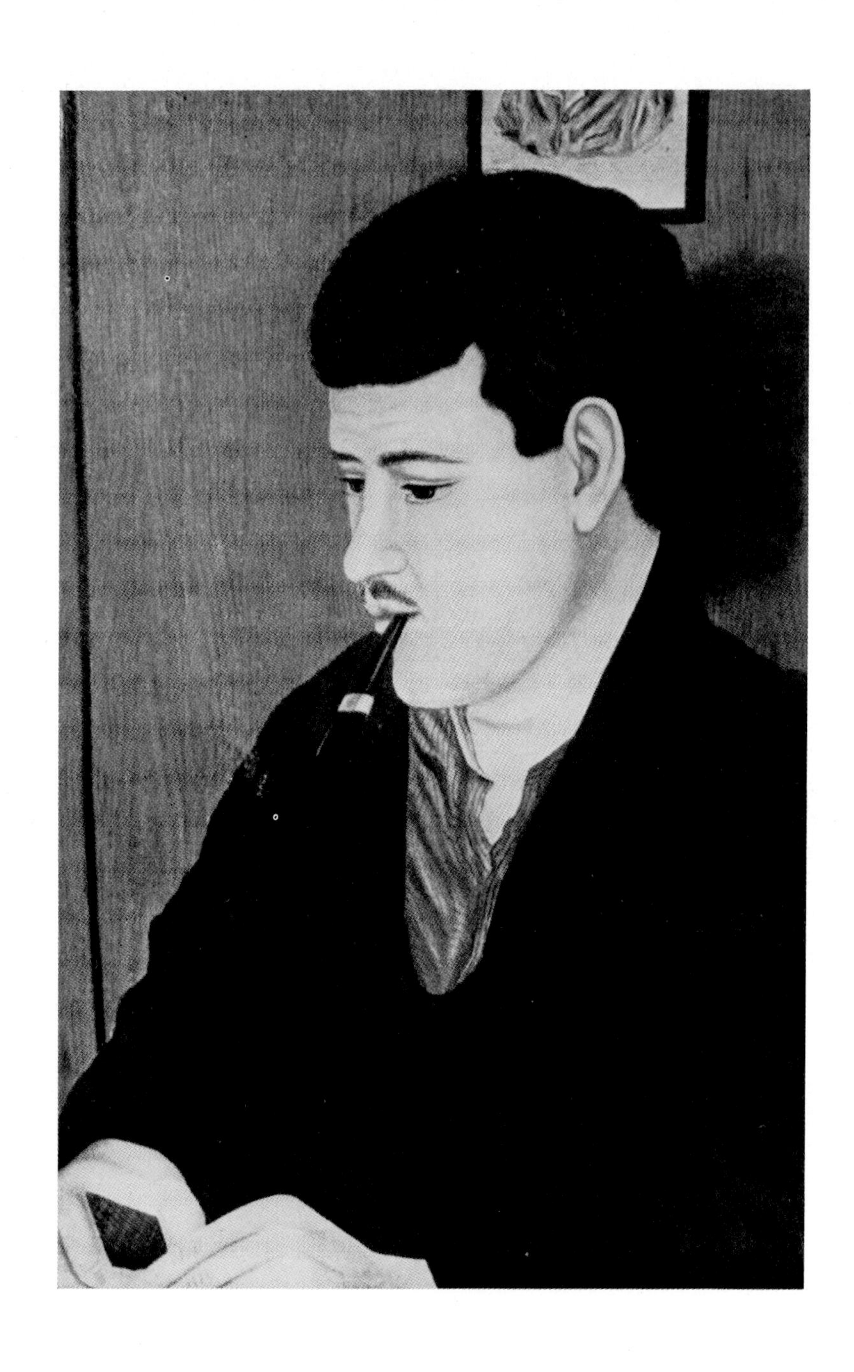

30 DIETRICH *Man with a Pipe*. 1926

31 DIETRICH *Foxes in the Forest.* 1923

36 DIETRICH *Morning on the Lake.* 1934

38 EVE *Boulevard Saint-Denis at Courbevoie*. 1937

40 EVE *Gypsy Encampment*. 1937

43 PEYRONNET *The Ferryman of the Moselle*

44 PEYRONNET *Forest Landscape*

47 PEYRONNET *The Model*

48 PEYRONNET *The Open Sea*

50 PEYRONNET *The Fields of Charente*

53 RIMBERT *Street Scene with Nun*. 1927

56 RIMBERT *Sunny Road at Perpézac-le-Noir.* 1930

58 RIMBERT *Morning in the Courtyard.* 1924

59 ROUSSEAU *Le Château Fort.* 1889

62 ROUSSEAU *Portrait of a Young Girl*

63 ROUSSEAU *Jungle*

64 ROUSSEAU *Jungle with Lions*

66 ROUSSEAU *Jungle with Two Monkeys.* 1900-1910

67 ROUSSEAU *The Umbrella*

ROUSSEAU *The Pink Candle*

ROUSSEAU *Still Life*

ROUSSEAU *Île de la Cité*

73 SÉRAPHINE *Cluster of Fruits*

74 SÉRAPHINE *Autumn Leaves*

82 VIVIN *Still Life with Oysters*

83 VIVIN *Quai de l'Horloge*

85 VIVIN *Place du Tertre in Winter*. 1929

87 VIVIN *Wild Boar Chased by Dogs*

89 VIVIN *Church Interior*

# *The American Artists*

# *Artists of the People*

OUR TIME has devoted so much fascinated attention to the subject of folk and popular art that it would seem, almost, that we had created it from the void by the very intensity of our interest. It does not take a great deal of investigation, however, to establish the fact that this art has an ancient and honorable lineage. Folk and popular art is very close to the sources of American expression. Splendid examples of it are in existence, from the work of the earliest anonymous limners of seventeenth century New England to the contemporary work displayed in this exhibition.

The discovery of this art of the people, as we find it illustrated in this exhibition, has been the work of our generation. It has often been said that America discovers herself anew every thirty years or so, and that in the process each generation rebels against its fathers in favor of its grandfathers. The discovery of the America which is represented by its folk and popular art has been a very slow process. Our generation, in discovering it, has rebelled not only against its fathers, but also against its grandfathers and great-grandfathers.

It is a curious fact that for a long time we believed in the possibility of American folklore, folk music and folk dance, while refusing to admit the possibility of an American folk and popular art. This was due, probably, to the obstinacy of thought-patterns. The usual conception of an art of the people is that of peasant art. It seems to be our idea that the European peasant, when he comes to these shores, changes at once into the American laborer, the American artisan or the American farmer. From that time no one would think of associating with him the idea of peasant expression.

But whether or not we have always believed in this art, it has existed in this country, as in most other countries, at the level of useful workmanship. It has been produced by shop-trained craftsmen and artisans who knew the meaning of sound construction and who wanted to "blend the useful with the agreeable" in their work. It has been produced by untrained workingmen, farmers and amateurs whose passion to construct a version of the outer world of fact, or to externalize a vision of the inner world of feeling, fantasy and idea, disciplined them to achieve mastery of a technique for setting down what they had to say.

It is evident that these artists came from many walks of life, but the kinds of art they produced are, basically, two: the art of the craftsman and the art of the amateur. On the one hand we have had the traditional work of the figurehead carver, on the other the tentative efforts of the village whittler. On the one hand we have had the sure, shop-trained work of the limner and the sign-painter, like Edward Hicks, on the other the less certain but no less interesting work of the amateur, like Joseph Pickett or John Kane. Of course men like Pickett and Kane were artisans who knew carpentry and this undoubtedly gave them the feeling for good joinery which their work shows so clearly. The folk and popular arts have always existed among these people in spite of the neglect of the fashionable art world. On more than one occasion the work of these artists of the common people has risen from the submerged esthetic channels of everyday life into the broad stream of art history. (Such artists in this exhibition as Edward Hicks, Joseph Pickett, T. A. Hoyer, Lawrence Lebduska, Vincent Canadé, Emile Branchard and Pedro Cervantez are certainly worthy of the attention of the art historian.)

The names of the artists represented in this exhibition are known to us, but most of the popular and folk artists of this country were anonymous. Among them were house and sign painters, shipwrights, carriage makers, carpenters, cabinet makers, wood and stone carvers, masons, plasterers, metal workers, blacksmiths, business and professional men, laborers, sailors and farmers. Edward Hicks was a carriage maker and painter. Joseph Pickett was a carpenter and builder of canal boats. Vincent Canadé worked as a plasterer. John Kane was a carpenter, house painter and mine and factory worker. Lawrence Lebduska began as a stained-glass worker. Emile Branchard was a workman. Patrick J. Sullivan is a house painter. T. A. Hoyer during most of his life was a vaudeville acrobat. Pedro Cervantez and Horace Pippin were workmen.

Very few of these artists have had any professional training or book learning in art. But they had the art of making things with their hands, an art which has declined rapidly with the progress of the machine age, and most of them have had the craftsman's respect for sound construction. In spite of the overwhelming prestige in our time of the idea of the-machine-as-creator, these people have refused to abandon to it, altogether, their form-creating function. Whether or not this traditional obstinacy of the hand-worker is important for society will appear only in the perspective of history. Certainly it should be one of the forces to be reckoned with in deciding whether or not the character of civilization in the future is to be dictated by the potentialities and limitations of the machine.

The work of these masters of folk and popular expression represents the survival of tastes and traditions which, as Fernand Léger has pointed out, "go back to the work of primitive and popular artists preceding the Renaissance." It has qualities which European and American art have been trying to recover for fifty years and more. It may be argued that some of these qualities result from technical inadequacy. But it is certain that there is much more to this work than mere lack of technical proficiency, and that in any event such criticism is narrowly academic. For upwards of two thousand years European criticism has recognized the fact that art is not necessarily identified with proficiency of material execution or perfection of finish. Criticism in our time has recognized that methods of execution often have more to do with intention than they have with mere facility, and that the methods of artists must differ as their aims differ. It would be ridiculous to expect a baroque artist to follow the linear methods of Dürer or Holbein, or to impose upon a master of Chinese landscape the methods of the Dutch or the mechanical and space-destroying perspective of a Gérôme.

It would be a mistake to apply naturalistic and academic standards to the work of these masters of popular art. And yet these artists may be called, as they have been called, "masters of reality." So far as realistic effect is concerned they are in harmony with the best contemporary practice. They are devoted to fact, as a thing to be known and respected, not necessarily as a thing to be imitated. Surface realism means nothing to these artists. With them realism becomes passion and not mere technique. They have set down what they saw, but, much more, they have set down what they knew and what they felt. Men like Pickett, Hoyer, Cervantez, Canadé, Branchard and Kane may be called masters of reality because their art is a response to the outside world of fact and they have very definite methods for its pictorial reconstruction.

It is remarkable what good technicians many of these painters are, and this is especially true of the shop-trained men of the past. The works of Edward Hicks, for instance, after the lapse of a hundred years, are in a better state of preservation than the works of many other painters of far greater reputation and, presumably, far greater technical knowledge. This is not surprising when one remembers that the tradition out of which the work of Edward Hicks came was in many respects not unlike that of the old masters. That is to say it was a tradition of craftsmanship which grew out of the handling of tools and materials, rather than an academic tradition passed on by art schools. It was not painting by the book or by theory.

Shop-trained men like Edward Hicks knew all about their materials, or at least as much as they needed to know as painters. Hicks undoubtedly ground his own colors and so was pretty sure of what he was getting. His methods were traditional and dependable. He knew his materials, probably made his own brushes and prepared his own painting grounds. None of these things would be true of the later folk artists, except possibly Joseph Pickett, who used house paint and a variety of other materials which he seems to have prepared himself. It is evident that Canadé, Branchard, Hoyer, Cervantez, Lebduska and the other contemporaries in this exhibition have followed, more or less, and so far as their knowledge and experience would permit, the methods of the average school-trained painter. But when one comes to examine their styles, even when these styles are extremely personal, one detects a certain kinship with the earlier folk artists and with the work of pre-Renaissance primitive and popular masters.

This kinship shows definitely in the work of Edward Hicks and Joseph Pickett. Pickett, who may be considered a contemporary (he died in 1918), shows it as clearly as Hicks. The work of these two men, which covers a period of more than a hundred years, presents some interesting comparisons and contrasts. Hicks was trained in the eighteenth century and was painting signs in the first decade of the nineteenth. Most of Pickett's work was done during the second decade of the twentieth century. Pickett was entirely self-taught as a painter and his work seems to be an expression of sheer genius. Hicks, on the other hand, was an artist-craftsman, thoroughly trained through a period of seven years' apprenticeship in the shop of a carriage-maker and painter. His work is of great interest to us, not only because of its quality, but also because we know a great deal about his training and ideas. We know, for instance, that his Quaker convictions, which were deep and sincere, did not interfere with his career as an artist. Hicks appears to have divided his life almost equally between preaching and painting. When he was not busy preaching or working in the sign shop he painted a number of allegorical and historical compositions, *The Peaceable Kingdom*, *The Grave of William Penn* and *Penn's Treaty with the Indians*, making several versions of each subject. Of *The Peaceable Kingdom* he is said to have painted forty versions.

What is there in the work of Hicks that relates it to the work of Pickett and the later contemporaries in this exhibition? One may say, of course, that it has the same fresh unexpectedness of personal style which in this kind of painting may be no more than an expression of naïveté. But there is something more. The freshness, the unexpectedness, appear to be the result of something which artists are always striving for—innocence and intensity of vision—far more than they are an expression of naïveté. And there is, too, something else here which is of great importance to the contemporary artist—structure as firm and logical as that of the carriages upon which Edward Hicks worked as an apprentice. The spatial arrangement in *The Grave of William Penn* (plate 119) is admirably clear. In *The Peaceable Kingdom* (plate 118) the painter has given us his version of the real world organized in a space which in certain parts of the picture recedes sharply into distance, but all is firmly controlled within the divisions of the two-dimensional space of the canvas. The deep vista at the left is coördinated with the rest of the picture so that it functions almost as an abstract element. It is this sort of control which the artist must establish if his space composition is to be more than the open-window view of the pedestrian landscape painter or the casual observer.

The work of Edward Hicks has compositional qualities of a high order. It shows innocence of vision and simplicity and freshness of expression, and it shows knowledge, too. The knowledge was limited to what Hicks had learned in the carriage shop, but it was a clear and well-tried knowledge, solidly founded in tradition and not in theory. In his mastery of his narrow range of knowledge, in the honesty and intensity of his vision and the religious sincerity which inspired his work, Hicks is akin to the great European primitives. He may be called an American Rousseau, who antedates the *douanier* by half a century.

Similar to the work of Hicks in its honesty, in its firm control of structure and its relevance to contemporary expression is the work of Joseph Pickett. He was a carpenter and storekeeper who, late in life, was seized with an ambition to paint the history of his native town. It is said that he made his own brushes and eked out his restricted palette with the juice of berries and the red clay of the Delaware river hills, improvising his technique and his tools as he went along. In some respects he drew like a child, but there is nothing childish or tentative about his way of constructing a picture. His training as an artisan had given him a respect for the physical reality of the painter's medium—the surface of his canvas and the pigment with which he worked. Possibly because he had this respect for the reality of his medium, and possibly because he knew no other way, when he wanted to achieve an effect of sculptural modeling he built up his forms in relief, sometimes nearly half an inch above the canvas.

In *Manchester Valley*, for instance, Pickett uses a variety of peculiarly personal methods. (See color plate, frontispiece.) There is a freely arbitrary handling of perspective. As a matter of fact there are several perspectives in *Manchester Valley*. The relationship of objects in space has been worked out from many points of view, and in addition one might say that the artist has established a temporal perspective, showing the landscape as he remembered it from acquaintance with its various aspects over a long period of time. There is very effective division of the space in a series of diagonals. The railroad, the fences and the trees not only divide the area of the picture in a most interesting way but they also set up spatial relationships as logical and satisfying as those which one might expect to find in the work of a master of Chinese landscape. All this, of course, is idiosyncratic, and peculiarly personal, but it shows a remarkable sense of design and craftsmanship of a very inventive kind. Everything is clearly stated, logically coördinated. Pickett's arbitrary handling of perspective, which enables him to make a complete statement concerning a landscape and, at the same time, hold the spatial organization firmly together, his sensitive and precise space division, his feeling for the right relation between areas of color and his ingenious methods for suggesting texture make him one of the most authentic and important of the masters of folk and popular art.

Pickett has the severity which one associates with primitives, and a similar quality appears in the painting of such artists as T. A. Hoyer, Vincent Canadé, Emile Branchard and Pedro Cervantez. In the work of Hoyer everything is neat and precisely controlled. The artist divides the areas of his canvas according to an exact and habitual method, marking off the divisions with great definiteness (for instance the sharply defined path of light in *Inside a Barn*, plate 128, and the divisions of *A Grazing Field*, plate 132). Each area is meticulously painted, usually in a painstaking one-color pointillism. This pointillist method is used to establish definite yet subtle boundaries between areas, to give variation of surface and to suggest recession of planes. Very rarely is it used as a pointillism of divided color and almost never for the purpose of color modeling. The method is precise to the point of obsession, and would have tried even the science and the patience of a Seurat. Curiously, it is not Seurat of whom Hoyer thinks as a forerunner but the Dutch masters, and, among American artists, George Inness.

Somewhat similar precision and severity appear in the work of Pedro Cervantez. Cervantez divides his work on a basically linear plan into areas of flat color as unrelieved as the cloudless skies of New Mexico. (Plates 104, 106, 107, 111.) Hoyer paints from memory. Cervantez works in direct response to his environment. The same things may be said of John Kane, who reacted with the simple-hearted affection of a child to the inspiration of his western Pennsylvania hillside towns which he set down with honesty and directness. Kane had the artisan's respect for the painter's medium and a good deal of feeling for surface and pattern. His color is often excellent. (Plates 137, 139, 143, 145, 147, 148, 149, 151, 153.) The work of the two Canadians, Chester Dalson (plate 114) and Robert Cauchon (plate 101) is amateur painting which has a good deal of vitality and charm and which appears to be a direct response to the inspiration of the country.

The other American painters in this exhibition, Vincent Canadé,

Emile Branchard, Lawrence Lebduska, Patrick J. Sullivan, "Pa" Hunt and Horace Pippin, appear, like Hoyer, to paint largely from memory. Canadé works like a primitive, especially in his severe, tragic portraits with their sense of diminished volume and frontal presentation of the mask. He has a fine sense of arrangement. (Plates 97, 98.) Lawrence Lebduska has the stylistic habits and the space organization of a primitive, but he has none of the acid severity of Canadé. Lebduska's work has the joyous emotional vitality and the decorative sense of peasant art. (Plates 156, 157, 158, 160.) Emile Branchard's work was lyrical and sensitive to a degree. It is vertical painting of a flat-pattern type which achieves interesting effects of decorative arrangement in such pictures as *Winter Night* (plate 92) and *The Struggle* (plate 96). When we come to "Pa" Hunt we are in an almost flat-patterned world with here and there the slightest linear suggestion of receding planes. (Plate 134.) Hunt is the naïve artist reacting directly to a world of optical space. With Horace Pippin we are in the field of the naïve and instinctive painter who struggles to invent symbols to express emotionally-felt visual memories. (Plates 165, 166.) Patrick J. Sullivan may be included among the group of instinctive painters. He presents in his paintings a complex of densely-packed personal meanings in which every object and every form has associative and symbolic values difficult for the spectator to appreciate. Many of these have been interpreted by the artist; others, perhaps, will be known in their full range only by the psychoanalyst. (Plates 169, 170.)

The work of these folk and popular artists has special significance for our generation because we have discovered that we can take seriously, once more, the idea of art for the people. This idea has gathered a good deal of energy in our time and has moved various groups in various ways—some to enthusiasm, others to satirical deprecation. From the beginning of the century up to the nineteen-twenties the phrase "art for the people" seemed to most critics almost a contradiction in terms, and for many it became an expression of contempt.

The high priests of this point of view were certain critics in London and Paris a decade or more ago. In their view the art experience seemed a rarefied activity, limited to a few individuals, the elect of art who are distinguished from the great mass of the non-elect by a special sensitiveness. This point of view, which amounts to a sort of esthetic Calvinism, still prevails in certain art circles in this country. It is, in the main, a collectors' or museum point of view and is not shared by many contemporary artists. During the past few years, and especially under the stimulus of their work on the government projects, the idea of art for the people has stirred large groups of American artists to enthusiasm. This enthusasm has been nourished by the discovery that our country has always had an art of the people, a popular and folk interest in painting and sculpture which has found spontaneous expression in the work of artisan, craftsman and amateur.

Folk and popular art is significant for us because, in our fear that contemporary civilization has almost abandoned its form-creating function in favor of the sterile mathematics of machine-form, we are startled and reassured to find this rich creativeness still alive in the unpretentious activities and avocations of the common man. It is significant, too, because in this art we find qualities sadly lacking in the internationalized academicism bequeathed to us by the nineteenth century—an academicism which raised the banner of its anaemic and philistine conception of form as the standard and ideal of universal art.

Because the art of the common man has this significance for us it is important that we value it with critical discrimination. Eager acceptance and overvaluation of its every manifestation is definitely a disservice to the cause of art. Naïve, amateur, popular and folk art is of no particular importance if it is merely the expression of a vague desire to engage in some sort of cultural activity, or if it is no more than a flawed image from the art of the past mirrored in the work of lesser artists today. But when it is the expression of unconscious talent that feels its way as unerringly as it does in the work of Joseph Pickett;

when it is a reflection of tradition refreshed and revitalized by the life experience of the people as it is in the work of Edward Hicks; when it is a communication in terms of the painter's medium of the ideas, the experience, the humor, the simple depth of feeling of the common man, as it is in the work of many of the contemporaries in this exhibition, then it may be of very great importance.

How are we to estimate the folk and popular art of America? How are we to judge these artists of the people? Judgments of relative value are difficult. Folk and popular art cannot, probably, be valued as highly as the work of our greatest masters, though many keen European and Mexican students would put men like Edward Hicks and Joseph Pickett not only in the front rank of the folk and popular artists of the past hundred years but also among the first half dozen masters of American painting. Whatever one thinks of these judgments there can be no question that these and many other artists of the people are entitled to an honorable place in the history of American painting. As their work becomes better known it should do much toward creating a better understanding of the American tradition in the arts and a richer interpretation of the cultural history of our country.

HOLGER CAHILL

# *Emile Branchard*

Emile Pierre Branchard was born of French parents in New York City in 1881. His stepfather was a painter who had been a pupil of Meissonier. Emile never had any art training but when he was a boy he used sometimes to watch his stepfather paint and think how he could probably do much better himself. He did not begin to paint, however, until about 1912, when he was over thirty years old. He painted simply for his own amusement.

Emile's mother had a rooming house in Washington Square South and in this house Emile lived for some fifty years. He worked at various jobs; for a while he was a truck driver and, at another time, a stevedore. During the World War he was on the Home Defense Force. In 1918 illness forced him to resign, and he found himself with time in which to take up painting seriously.

Branchard is said to have painted only from memory, and the landscapes with trees which were his favorite subject were based upon memories of a summer spent in Connecticut when he was twelve or thirteen years of age. He first exhibited with the Society of Independent Artists in New York in 1919. After his "discovery" at the Independents' his work was exhibited regularly from 1919 to 1932 at the gallery of Stephan Bourgeois. Branchard died in New York in February, 1938.

D. C. M.

*92 WINTER NIGHT
Oil on canvas, 13 x 16 inches

93 SILVERY NOON
Oil on canvas, 16⅛ x 12⅛ inches

94 WINTER
Oil on canvas, 25⅛ x 18⅛ inches

95 WOODLAND
Oil on canvas, 25⅛ x 18⅛ inches

*96 THE STRUGGLE
Oil on composition board, 24 x 18⅛ inches

Nos. 92-96 lent by Mrs. Emile Branchard, New York

# *Vincent Canadé*

Vincent Canadé was born in 1879 at Cosenza, Italy. When he was a boy his family lost their money, sold their land and came to New York. Vincent was twelve years old when he was sent out to earn his living. During the years that followed he tried his hand at many trades, never very successfully, always interested only in painting. It seems that he went to art school but only for one day. A jeweler who employed him sent him to study ornament at Cooper Union, but the class did not interest him and after the first day he never went back. He worked as a barber and then as a plasterer and house painter, managing always to earn only a bare existence for himself and his family.

Around 1918 the pictures which Canadé had painted over a period of years came to the attention of the public through the interest of Joseph Stella, who may be said to have discovered Canadé. Since that time Canadé's work has been included in many exhibitions. Canadé is represented by paintings in the collections of the Phillips Memorial Gallery, the Newark Museum, the Whitney Museum of American Art, the Museum of Modern Art, and his work is also included in a number of private collections.

D. C. M.

*97 DOUBLE SELF PORTRAIT. 1923
Oil on wood, 9½ x 7⅛ inches
Lent by E. Weyhe, New York

*98 THE ARTIST'S FAMILY. About 1924
Oil on canvas, 28½ x 21 inches
Lent by the Weyhe Gallery, New York

99 SELF PORTRAIT. About 1926
Oil on composition board, 18⅝ x 14 inches
The Museum of Modern Art, gift of Mrs. John D. Rockefeller, Jr.

100 THE TOWN BY A RIVER
Oil on canvas, 30 x 24 inches
Lent by the Phillips Memorial Gallery, Washington, D. C.

# *Robert Cauchon*

Robert Cauchon lives at La Malbaie, Murray Bay, in the Province of Quebec. He was born in 1915. His father is a blacksmith and a carriage and sleigh maker. Robert began studying for the priesthood but gave this up because of ill health. He now works in his father's shop, and paints in the evenings and on Sundays. He likes best to paint horses in action, pulling carriages and sleighs, and the blacksmith's shop has given him an intimate knowledge of his favorite subject matter.

D. C. M.

*101 THE RED SURREY
Gouache, 14¾ x 22 inches
Lent by Mr. and Mrs. Wendell Davis, New York

102 OX IN HARNESS
Gouache
Lent by Patrick Morgan, New York

103 RETURNING FROM MASS IN WINTER
Gouache
Lent by Mrs. C. K. Post, New York

# *Pedro Cervantez*

Pedro Cervantez was born in Arizona in 1915. He has often remarked that he would like to visit the town in which he was born if he only knew its name. His maternal grandparents were potters in Gomez Palacio, Durango, Mexico. During a revolution their kiln and pottery shop were destroyed, and about 1914 the family came to the United States to join relatives who had emigrated before them. Pedro's father works as a section hand for the Santa Fe Railroad and lives in the town of Texico, New Mexico. Pedro had apparently never thought of using a family name until someone suggested that he sign the first painting he exhibited. Then, instead of taking his mother's name in accordance with the usual custom of his people, he took his father's name, because he had been told of an earlier Cervantes who was a great man.

Pedro Cervantez is self taught, except for various "correspondence courses" in art, which have not managed to warp his native abilities. R. Vernon Hunter, director of the Federal Art Project in New Mexico, and "discoverer" of Cervantez, tells the story of how the boy started to paint: "The first time I saw Cervantez he was in the corner drug store. . . . From memory I did a small color sketch of him. Someone told him about it, and he came to the studio to see it. He kept coming back daily for several weeks, silently watching me paint. One day he appeared with a group of sketches over which I was most enthusiastic. He said he had often thought it would be nice to make pictures, but he had not known how to go about it."

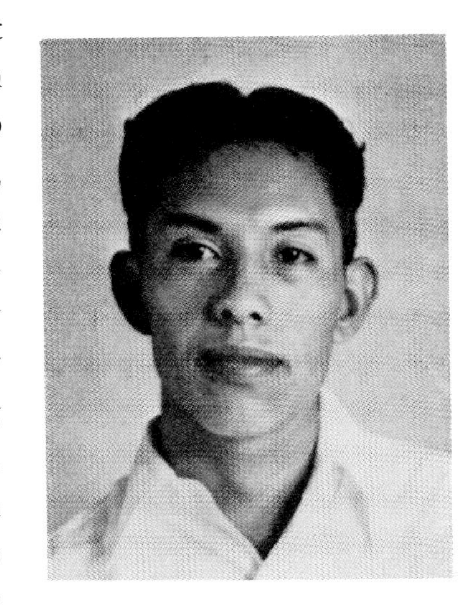

Two months later one of Cervantez' paintings was sent to the Fiesta Show at Santa Fe, New Mexico, and was bought by the painter, Josef Bakos. Since that time Cervantez has never wavered in his determination to paint. He works very slowly, pondering things as he goes along, and he shows a great eagerness to learn. He is at present employed on the WPA Federal Art Project in New Mexico.

D. C. M.

*104 CROQUET GROUND. 1936
Oil on composition board, 19¾ x 28¾ inches

105 PIGEONS. 1936
Oil on composition board, 19½ x 15¼ inches

*106 PANHANDLE LUMBER COMPANY. 1937
Oil on composition board, 17½ x 24⅛ inches

*107 PINK OXALIS ON STOVE. 1937
Oil on composition board, 26½ x 15¼ inches

108 STOVE. 1937
Oil on composition board, 19 x 14 inches

109 RAILROAD STATION, TEXICO, NEW MEXICO. 1937
Oil on composition board, 24½ x 28¾ inches

110 RAILROAD SEMAPHORE. 1937
Oil on composition board, 25¾ x 16 inches

*111 CUATES PRIVADAS. 1937
Oil on composition board, 14¾ x 19¾ inches

112 BOVINA ELEVATOR. 1937
Oil on composition board, 27¼ x 21 inches

113 LILIES. 1937
Oil on composition board, 24 x 20 inches

Nos. 104-113 lent by the New Mexico Federal Art Project of the Works Progress Administration

# *Chester Dalson*

Chester Dalson was born in Canada, probably about 1906. His mother was English and his father Scandinavian. His mother painted, and although she died when Dalson was a small child her painting made a deep impression upon him and he wanted to carry it on. He worked as a laborer, sometimes in the United States, sometimes in Canada, and painted continually in his spare time. He never had any training in painting and had little or no acquaintance with original works of art.

In 1936, when the landscapes listed below were painted, Dalson was working in a lumber mill at Melanson, a hamlet near Wolfville, Nova Scotia. At the end of that summer he left Melanson and has not been heard of since.

(This information has been supplied by Mr. Walter Abell, of the Brooklyn Museum, who knew Dalson and has lent his pictures for this exhibition.)

D. C. M.

*114 LANDSCAPE. 1936
Oil on cardboard, 18¾ x 28¼ inches
Lent by Walter Abell, Brooklyn, N. Y.

115 LANDSCAPE WITH CARIBOU. 1936
Oil on cardboard, 9¾ x 22 inches
Lent by Walter Abell, Brooklyn, N. Y.

# *Edward Hicks*

Edward Hicks was a Quaker preacher who made his living as a coach maker and painter, and as a house and sign painter. He painted signs for inns, shops, roads and bridges, made fire screens and is said to have done portraits. When he was not busy preaching or working at his trade, he painted allegorical and historical pictures, making a number of versions of each subject. His favorite subjects were *The Peaceable Kingdom*, *Penn's Treaty with the Indians* and *The Grave of William Penn.*

Hicks was a deeply religious man. He preached at Quaker meetings in Pennsylvania, Maryland, New York, Ohio, Indiana and Canada. In 1825, with his cousin Elias Hicks of Jericho, Long Island, founder of the Hicksite sect of Quakers, he preached at Quaker meeting-houses in Rose and Hester Streets in New York. These sermons were published under the title of *Sermons Delivered by Elias Hicks and Edward Hicks in Friends' Meetings, New York, in the 5th Month, 1825*. A book of his memoirs was published in Philadelphia in 1851. He also published a number of pamphlets of religious discourses, among them *A Little Present for Friends and Friendly People in the Form of a Miscellaneous Discourse by a Poor Illiterate Mechanic and A Work of Exhortation to Young Friends. Presented to Them Without Money and Without Price. By a Poor Illiterate Minister.* His memoirs are filled with religious exhortations and the most truly pious sentiment. His work as a painter is rarely mentioned.

Edward Hicks was born at Attleborough, Bucks County, Pennsylvania, on April 4, 1780. He was a descendant of Robert Hicks who landed at Plymouth in 1621 on the *Fortune*, the ship which followed the *Mayflower*. His parents died when he was very young, and it is said that for some time he was cared for by a Negro woman who had been a servant of the family. Later he was adopted by David and Elizabeth Twining. His painting of the Twining home (plate 122) is evidently intended to represent it as it appeared in 1787 when Hicks was a child of seven. The Twining family were all devout Quakers and the child was brought up in that faith.

At the age of thirteen Hicks was apprenticed to a coach maker named Tomlinson at Four-Lanes-End near Attleborough. He remained there for seven years, learning the coach making trade, and especially the painting of coaches. He came to the shop a very pious boy. But, he says: "The tenderness of my religious impressions too soon wore off, and instead of weeping and praying I soon got to laughing and swearing; and having what may truly be called a natural fund of nonsense I soon became a favorite with my shop mates." In 1800, after his seven years' apprenticeship had been completed, Hicks got his first job: to make a coach for a Doctor Featon and to paint his house. While he was engaged on this job, a serious illness caused him to turn anew to religion, and he started to attend Quaker meetings again. It was said of him that he "was favored with a renewed visitation of Heavenly love; and yielding thereto he passed through the dispensation of condemnation, which he viewed as baptism unto repentance, by which his former pleasures were marred, and the friendship and glory of the world were stained in his view.... About the 30th year of his age he came into the ministry, deeply in the cross to his natural will . . . covering the meetings with that solemnity which is precious and comforting to those present. . . ."

In 1801 Hicks moved to Milford and went into partnership with Joshua C. Canby. In 1803 he was received into the Society of Friends, and in the same year was married to Miss Sarah Worstal. A few months later the partnership with Canby was dissolved. Hicks built himself a house in Milford in which he and his wife lived until 1811 when they moved to Newtown. Newtown at that time had no meeting house, and, as Hicks says, "comparatively speaking, every tenth house was a tavern." A Friends' meeting house was built at Newtown a few years after Hicks' arrival there and he became its minister. "Being fruitful he grew in his gift and became an eminent minister of the Gospel; adorning the doctrine he preached by a life corresponding therewith." During his ministry he labored "with his hands for the support of his family, so that he could say with the apostle, 'these hands have ministered to my necessities and those that were with me.' "

In 1813 Hicks began to travel about to Philadelphia, Baltimore and other neighboring towns to preach at Quaker meetings. So much of his time was spent away from home that his trade was neglected. In order to relieve his financial situation he temporarily abandoned painting for farming. The farming was a failure, however, and he had to return to his old trade, even though he considered farming more consistent with the Christian life and, as he says, "was willing to sacrifice all my fondness for painting." In his *Memoirs* he wrote: "If the Christian world was in the real spirit of Christ, I do not believe there would be such a fine thing as a painter in Christendom. It appears to me to be one of those trifling, insignificant arts, which has never been of any substantial advantage to mankind. But as the inseparable companion of voluptuousness and pride, it has presaged the downfall of empires and kingdoms, and in my view stands now enrolled among the premonitory symptoms of the rapid decline of the American Republic." In spite of these ideas Hicks was too much interested in his work ever to desert his easel. In continuing his worldly art of painting Hicks was encouraged by his Quaker friends, one of whom said to him: "Edward, thee has now a source of independence within thyself, in thy peculiar talent for painting. Keep to it within the bounds of innocence and usefulness, and thee can always be comfortable."

It is said that at one time there was scarcely a tavern in Bucks County which did not have a sign painted by Hicks. Shortly after his arrival at Newtown Hicks got an order to paint an inn sign showing the proprietor driving his coach-and-four. When the inn keeper saw his new sign he was very much disappointed. "That man on the box looks as if he were drunk," he told the painter. Hicks replied, "Thee is usually that way and I wanted it to look natural." After the proprietor promised to try not to be drunk while driving his coach, Hicks repainted the sign.

During the last ten or fifteen years of his life, although he was still active as a minister, Hicks spent more and more time in his shop, painting. His diary, which he kept from 1846 until his death in 1849, is full of entries such as these: "Steadily engaged in my shop. My business, though too trifling and insignificant for a Christian to follow, affords me an honorable and I hope honest living. Having to work with my own hands, for all the money I get, appears to me to be more in accordance with primitive Christianity, than living on the work of other people's hands. . . ." "Engaged in my shop, working with my own hands and minding my own business. . . ." "Diligently employed in my shop, but not sufficiently devout. How true is the saying, 'Ye cannot serve God and Mammon.' " "In my shop. It seems a pity that my business should be of such a character as to be of no real use to anybody but myself, being the only way I can get an honest living." One entry in the diary reads: "Had another evidence of the important truth that like will beget its like. I took a sign, which I had painted, to a storekeeper, and told him my price, but observed that I was afraid it was too much and if he thought so I would take less. The storekeeper paid me cheerfully, only manifesting a fear that I had charged too little. Ah! there is such a thing as dealing on Christian principles, there is such a thing as doing right and being happy in this world."

A short time before his death Hicks told a friend that he was about to die. "My impression is that I shall go suddenly, without much pain or suffering, and with very little warning to my family." He was in his shop the entire day before he died, finishing a *Peaceable Kingdom* which he was painting for his daughter Elizabeth. On returning home he told his family that he believed he had paid his last visit to his shop. The next morning his daughter observed " 'she thought him better.' He replied he was better, he was comfortable, but requested they would not flatter themselves for he was going to die." The next day he was unable to attend meeting, and that evening, August 23, 1849, he died. He is buried at Newtown.

Edward Hicks' paintings are owned by members of the Hicks family, by the Friends' Home at Newtown, the Worcester Museum, the Doylestown Museum, the American Folk Art Gallery, and a number of private collectors. The Hicks family owns a portrait of him by his cousin Thomas Hicks, the portrait painter, who began as an apprentice at coach painting in Edward Hicks' shop.

D. C. M.

116 THE PEACEABLE KINGDOM
Oil on canvas, 25½ x 29½ inches
Lent anonymously

117 THE PEACEABLE KINGDOM
Oil on canvas, 17½ x 23 inches
Lent by the American Folk Art Gallery, New York

*118 THE PEACEABLE KINGDOM
Oil on canvas, 16⅝ x 20⅞ inches
Lent anonymously, courtesy the American Folk Art Gallery, New York

*119 THE GRAVE OF WILLIAM PENN. 1847
Oil on canvas, 24 x 30 inches

120 LANDSCAPE
Oil on wood, 16¾ x 20 inches
Nos. 119-120 lent by Mrs. John D. Rockefeller, Jr., courtesy the Ludwell-Paradise House, Williamsburg, Va.

121 CERES
Oil on wood, 18⅞ x 13½ inches
Lent by Mrs. Edith G. Halpert, New York

*122 THE RESIDENCE OF DAVID TWINING IN 1787
Oil on canvas, 26½ x 31½ inches
Collection Mrs. John D. Rockefeller, Jr. *Illustrated but not in the exhibition*

122A THE PEACEABLE KINGDOM
Oil on canvas
Lent by Miss Cornelia Carle Hicks, Newtown, Pennsylvania

122B NIAGARA FALLS
Oil on wood (fire-screen)
Lent by Edward N. Barnsley, Newtown, Pennsylvania

# *Thorvald Arenst Hoyer*

Thorvald Arenst Hoyer was born in Copenhagen in 1872, the son of a well-to-do coal dealer. He started to draw at the age of seven, and at thirteen entered the studio of the Danish painter, Frants Henningsen. For six years he was apprentice, rather than pupil, in Henningsen's studio, cleaning brushes and doing other chores and occasionally posing for child heads. When Henningsen discovered that the boy had talent, he advised him to travel and, particularly, to see the great museums of the world.

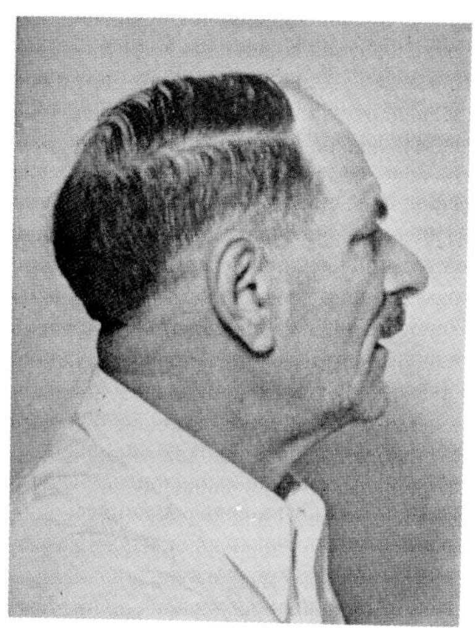

At the age of nineteen Hoyer started out to see the world. He had always been a strong and athletic boy, and he and a friend now teamed up as acrobats and toured Denmark and Germany. This was the beginning of a vaudeville career which lasted for twenty-four years and took Hoyer all over the world. With his first partner and four others he played in the music halls of Germany, France, Spain, Italy, England and Scandinavia, and then toured South Africa, India, Australia and the Americas. In 1902, during this tour, Hoyer performed in Chicago, the city which he later chose for his home.

Hoyer was what is known technically as an "understander," the man in the human pyramid who stands on the floor and supports the other acrobats on his shoulders. After his first team split up Hoyer became "understander" for the Yoskary Brothers, an Italian team remembered by vaudeville fans. He closed his stage career in 1915, and settled down to devote himself to painting.

During all his active career Hoyer's intense interest in art never wavered. He spent his spare time sketching and painting. He visited over and over again the great museums of Europe, and boasts that he has seen "every famous picture in the world." He feels that his own painting is in the tradition of the old masters. His particular hero, however, is George Inness, and he says: "I understand Inness as if I were his son."

At the Chicago World's Fair Hoyer had a small booth on the Fair grounds where he exhibited his paintings. However, his work was known to very few people until 1936. In that year he had his first one-man exhibition at the Findlay Galleries in Chicago under the sponsorship of a group called the Neoterics. He is now employed on the WPA Federal Art Project in Illinois.

(The Museum of Modern Art is indebted to Mr. C. J. Bulliet, art editor of the *Chicago Daily News*, for most of the above information, which appeared during 1936 in his column.)

D. C. M.

123 EARLY MORNING IN TEXAS. 1921
Oil on canvas, 17 x 21¼ inches
Lent by the artist

124 MOUNTAIN ROAD, KENTUCKY. 1930
Oil on canvas, 9¼ x 12⅛ inches
Lent by the artist

125 DRIFTING CLOUD. 1937
Oil on canvas, 14⅛ x 12¼ inches
Lent by the artist

126 AWAKEN. 1937
Oil on canvas, 12¼ x 10¾ inches
Lent by the artist

127 DOWN THE PECOS RIVER, TEXAS. 1936
Oil on canvas, 30¼ x 24¼ inches

*128 INSIDE A BARN. 1937
Oil on canvas, 30¼ x 24¼ inches

129 BLACK HILLS, SOUTH DAKOTA. 1937
Oil on canvas, 30¼ x 24¼ inches

130 EASTER SUNRISE. 1937
Oil on canvas, 30 x 24⅛ inches

131 ROCKY MOUNTAINS, MONTANA. 1937
Oil on canvas, 28¼ x 22⅛ inches

*132 A GRAZING FIELD. 1937
Oil on canvas, 30⅛ x 24 inches

*133 FOREST FIRE. 1937
Oil on canvas, 24¼ x 30¼ inches

Nos. 127-133 lent by the Illinois Federal Art Project of the Works Progress Administration

# *"Pa" Hunt*

"Pa" Hunt was born in New York in 1870. He went to live in Provincetown, Massachusetts, about 1930. At the age of sixty he painted his first picture on a piece of sheeting tacked into an old picture frame. From that time until his death in 1934 he was a well known figure in the art colony at Provincetown.

D. C. M.

*134 PETER HUNT'S ANTIQUE SHOP
Oil on canvas, 20 x 30 inches
Lent by Peter Hunt, Provincetown, Massachusetts

135 RUE DU BAC
Oil on cotton cloth, 23⅞ x 17⅞ inches
Lent by Peter Hunt, Provincetown, Massachusetts

# *John Kane*

John Kane was born in 1860 in West Calder, near Edinburgh, Scotland, one of a family of nine children. His parents had come from County Galway, Ireland. When he was nine years old he went to work in the coal mines of Scotland. He worked in the mines until he was nineteen. Then he came to America, to Pittsburgh, which had at that time the largest Scotch population of any city except Edinburgh. For years Kane worked in the furnaces at McKeesport, Connellsville and Bessemer, and for seven years thereafter he laid cobblestones in the streets of Pittsburgh. Then he went to work for the Pressed Steel Car Company. During his lunch hour he used to paint pictures on the cars for the amusement of his fellow workers. One day the superintendent caught him, but instead of firing him he advised him to take up art. After this Kane took up sign and house painting and carpentry.

Kane had always wanted to go to art school. In his sixties he started to paint on canvas, setting down for his own amusement the slum and factory scenes which he saw from his tenement window in the "Strip" section of Pittsburgh. Sometimes he went into the country, but the

Photograph from *Sky Hooks,* by John Kane, as told to Marie McSwigan. To be published by J. B. Lippincott.

city and its environs furnished most of his subject matter. He liked to paint pictures of the Scottish festivals at Kennywood.

In 1926 Kane first submitted a painting to the Carnegie International Exhibition in Pittsburgh. It was rejected. In 1927, however, his *Scene from the Scottish Highlands* passed the Carnegie jury, and Kane emerged from obscurity—the only Pittsburgh artist to exhibit that year. This painting was purchased by Andrew Dasburg, the painter, who was a member of the jury and winner of the third prize. The next year Kane won first prize at the Pittsburgh Artists' Annual Exhibition. Before his death he had several one-man exhibitions in New York and in Pittsburgh. In August, 1934, John Kane died of tuberculosis in a Pittsburgh hospital.

Once, when Kane was asked why he painted, he answered: "I like the puttin' on o' the color." And again, he said: "With art comes goodness and beauty."

E. VAN H.

136 ESCAPE. 1928
Oil on canvas, 22½ x 27½ inches
Lent by the Valentine Gallery, New York

*137 SELF PORTRAIT. 1929
Oil on panel, 36 x 27 inches
Collection the Valentine Gallery, New York. *Illustrated but not in the exhibition*

138 ACROSS THE "STRIP." 1929
Oil on canvas, 32¼ x 34¼ inches
Lent by the Phillips Memorial Gallery, Washington, D. C.

*139 BROTHER PATRICK IN UNIFORM OF THE BLACK WATCH
Oil on canvas, 72 x 30 inches
Lent by the Valentine Gallery, New York

140 LASSIE
Oil on canvas, 34 x 24 inches
Lent by the Valentine Gallery, New York

141 SCENE FROM THE SCOTTISH HIGHLANDS
Oil on canvas, 21½ x 25½ inches
Lent by Andrew Dasburg, courtesy the Walker Galleries, New York

142 THE GIRL I LEFT BEHIND
Oil on canvas, 16¼ x 13¼ inches
Lent by Mr. and Mrs. William Averell Harriman, New York

*143 ANDREW CARNEGIE'S BIRTHPLACE
Oil on canvas, 16 x 20 inches
Lent by the Valentine Gallery, New York

144 MT. MERCY ACADEMY
Oil on canvas, 20 x 24 inches
Lent by the Valentine Gallery, New York

*145 OLD ST. PATRICK'S
Oil on canvas, 24 x 28 inches
Lent anonymously

146 ST. PAUL'S CHURCH
Oil on canvas, 16 x 20 inches
Lent by Miss Adelaide Milton de Groot, courtesy the Metropolitan Museum of Art, New York

*147 TURTLE CREEK VALLEY
Oil on canvas, 34 x 44 inches
Lent by Henry R. Luce, New York

*148 HOMESTEAD
Oil on canvas, 24¼ x 26⅞ inches
The Museum of Modern Art, gift of Mrs. John D. Rockefeller, Jr.

*149 ALONG THE SUSQUEHANNA
Oil on canvas
Lent by Mr. and Mrs. William S. Paley, New York

150 MONONGAHELA RIVER VALLEY. 1931
Oil on canvas, 28 x 38 inches
Lent by Miss Adelaide Milton de Groot, New York

*151 FROM MY STUDIO WINDOW. 1932
Oil on canvas, 22¼ x 34½ inches
Lent by Miss Adelaide Milton de Groot, New York

152 PROSPERITY'S INCREASE. 1933
Oil on canvas, 32 x 40 inches
Lent by Mr. and Mrs. William S. Paley, New York

*153 TOUCHING UP. About 1934
Oil on canvas, 21 x 27 inches
Lent by the Valentine Gallery, New York

154 JOHN KANE AND HIS WIFE
Oil on canvas
Lent by the Valentine Gallery, New York

155 SCHENLEY MANSION
Oil on canvas, 18 x 36 inches
Lent by the Valentine Gallery, New York

# *Lawrence Lebduska*

Lawrence Lebduska was born of Bohemian parents in Baltimore, Maryland, in 1894. His father was a stained-glass maker. In 1899 Lawrence was taken to Europe. He was educated in Leipzig, learning the stained-glass craft at the Chemical and Technical School of Fleider and Schneider, which he attended for four years. Then he won a prize at an international art exposition at Leipzig for a painting called *Bit of Bohemia.* Later he studied for two years with Josef Svoboda in Chrudim, Bohemia, Czechoslovakia.

In 1912, when he was eighteen, Lebduska returned to the United States, going first to Baltimore and, a year later, to New York. His first job in New York was painting decorative murals for the firm of Elsie de Wolfe. During the years which followed he made stained glass and mural paintings for many New York houses, continuing his own painting in his spare time. He had his first one-man exhibition at the New York gallery, Contemporary Arts, in 1936. At present he is employed on the WPA Federal Art Project in New York.

D. C. M.

*156 EVE. 1936
Oil on canvas, 40 x 30 inches
Lent by H. Leonard Simmons, New York

*157 THE MONASTERY FARM, RHODE ISLAND. 1936
Oil on canvas, 28 x 38 inches

*158 BOHEMIAN KITCHEN. 1936
Oil on composition board, 24⅛ x 17⅞ inches

159 AFRICAN VILLAGE. 1936
Oil on canvas, 24 x 30 inches

*160 WHITE BELT CATTLE. 1937
Oil on canvas, 24 x 30 inches

161 THE MARKET. 1937
Oil on canvas, 16 x 20 inches

Nos. 157-161 lent by Contemporary Arts, New York

# *Joseph Pickett*

Joseph Pickett spent his life in the town of New Hope, Pennsylvania. He was born there in 1848. Like the rest of his family he was a carpenter and canal boat builder. Late in life he kept a little country grocery store on the banks of the Delaware Canal. He died in 1918 at New Hope and is buried in the nearby town of Hulmeville, Pennsylvania.

Pickett began to paint late in life. His ambition was to paint the history of his native town. The building in which he kept his grocery store is still standing, and on its front wall, under a layer of stucco now partially removed, is Pickett's first attempt at painting. The three large canvases listed in this catalog are the only oil paintings which Pickett is known to have made; at any rate they are the only paintings by him so far discovered. A few of his small sketches are in the possession of members of his family.

Pickett used to exhibit his paintings in the window of his grocery store. In 1918, the year he died, he was persuaded by a resident of the artist colony at New Hope to send a picture (probably *Manchester Valley*) to the Pennsylvania Academy's annual exhibition in Philadelphia. The painting was rejected but it is said to have received three jury votes, those of William L. Lathrop, Robert Henri and Robert Spencer. After Pickett's death his paintings were put up at auction, but as they brought only a dollar each his widow bought them in and gave *Manchester Valley* to the New Hope High School, where it hung for ten or twelve years. (The school is the large building with a flag shown in the painting.)

Relatives and neighbors of Pickett's in New Hope remember little about him. New Hope artists who knew him say he was the typical American artisan, uneducated except in his trade. He was never taught even the rudiments of art, but invented his technique and devised his tools and materials as he went along. He made his own brushes and used ordinary house paint which he mixed with sand, earth, rocks and shells in an effort to reproduce textures, an effort in which he succeeded remarkably well. He is said to have spent a great deal of time on each painting.

(The Museum of Modern Art is indebted for the above information to Mr. Holger Cahill, who introduced Pickett's work to the public in a series of museum exhibitions.)

D. C. M.

*162 MANCHESTER VALLEY.
Probably 1914-1918
Oil on canvas, 45 x 60 inches
Inscribed: *Jos. Pickett Art. Manchester Valley, New Hope, Pa.*
Lent by Mrs. John D. Rockefeller, Jr., New York

*Frontispiece*

*163 WASHINGTON UNDER THE COUNCIL TREE
Probably 1914-1918
Oil on canvas, 35 x 37½ inches
Lent by the Newark Museum, Newark, New Jersey

*164 CORYELL'S FERRY, 1776, AND WASHINGTON TAKING VIEWS
Probably 1914-1918
Oil on canvas, 38 x 48 inches
Collection the Whitney Museum of American Art, New York. *Illustrated but not in the exhibition*

# *Horace Pippin*

Horace Pippin is a disabled Negro war veteran who lives in West Chester, Pennsylvania. He was born in West Chester in 1888, and was brought up in Goshen, New York. When he was ten years old he answered the advertisement of an art supplies concern and received a box of colored crayons with which he made pictures of religious subjects. At fifteen he had to leave school to go to work. He worked for seven years as a hotel porter, then got a job in a storage warehouse in Patterson, New Jersey. He had several other jobs before 1917 when he enlisted in the Army and was sent to France. A year later he was badly wounded, was sent back to America, and in 1919 honorably discharged. He says of himself at this time: "Then I began to think of the things that I had always loved to do. First I got together all the old cigar boxes that I could get, and made fancy boxes out of them. . . . I was not satisfied with that sort of work. In the winter of 1925 I made my first burnt wood panels. . . . This brought me back to my old self." He began to paint in 1930, spending three years on his first painting. Pippin's work was discovered by Dr. Christian Brinton, who arranged an exhibition for him at the West Chester Community Center in 1937.

The following paragraph is quoted from a brief note by Horace Pippin:

"*How I Paint. . . .* The colors are very simple such as brown, amber, yellow, black, white and green. The pictures which I have already painted come to me in my mind, and if to me it is a worth while picture, I paint it. I go over that picture in my mind several times and when I am ready to paint it I have all the details that I need. I take my time and examine every coat of paint carefully and to be sure that the exact color which I have in mind is satisfactory to me. Then I work my foreground from the background. That throws the background away from the foreground. In other words bringing out my work. The time it takes to make a picture depends on the nature of the picture. For instance the picture called *The Ending of the War, Starting Home* which was my first picture. On that picture I couldn't do what I really wanted to do, but my next pictures I am working my thought more perfectly. My opinion of art is that a man should have love for it, because my idea is that he paints from his heart and mind. To me it seems impossible for another to teach one of Art."

D. C. M.

*165 SHELL HOLES AND OBSERVATION BALLOON, CHAMPAGNE SECTOR
Oil on muslin, 25 x 33¾ inches

*166 THE END OF THE WAR: STARTING HOME
Oil on canvas, 25 x 32½ inches

167 CABIN IN THE COTTON
Oil on muslin, 18 x 32¾ inches

168 THE BLUE TIGER
Oil on canvas, 16¼ x 27½ inches

Nos. 165-168 lent by the artist

# *Patrick J. Sullivan*

My first contact with the work of P. J. Sullivan, an unknown artist, left me profoundly impressed with the qualities of the man as a painter. *Man's Procrastinating Pastime*, his only completed work at the time, as I learned from subsequent correspondence, revealed through a deeply felt personal symbolism, a plastic maturity which the artist used to the fullest to express a dramatic intensity of conviction.

In contrast with the assertive quality of his paintings, his letters are those of a gentle philosophical soul, full of an unspoiled culture which directs his impulses towards simple human good. "To make people think," he has repeatedly written, "is my main reason for painting." In this quiet verbal expression is contained the zeal which conveys itself with such emotional force through his paintings.

The written "theme," as he calls it, which he has felt should accompany each picture, is conceived together with the title as an extension of the painting itself, and discloses the underlying symbolism. Each character and each object is identified and extensively described in its relation to the very seriously thought-out thematic development in all three of his paintings.

In *Man's Procrastinating Pastime*, "the forest is the subconscious mind of man. . . . The man kneeling over the grave symbolizes mankind in general burying the evil part of himself deep in the mind. . . . The tall, formidable-looking man is urging mankind to get out into the conscious or clear light of day. . . . The grotesque creature to the right is my personification of sin . . ." and he amplifies this, detail upon detail, leading to the summation that "man is always procrastinating, trying to hide his evil self instead of courageously showing his good part and performing good deeds—hence the title."

*An Historical Event*, his second work, is an interpretation of the "Wallis-Edward" romance. "The picture as a whole is the heart of the ex-king . . ." from which "Cupid is ordering the lion with its empire representations. . . ." Because of the artist's integrity of spirit, the picture is far removed from the easy sentimentality with which a lesser intuition might have invested it.

In his third painting, *A Rendezvous with the Soul*, he returns again to abstract contemplation. "The earth is man's life. . . . It is autumn, the end of the season. The sun is gone, the end of the day. The very aged man is at the end of his life. . . . The spiritual fire around the soul indicates the despair and suffering man experiences in dying. . . ."

Patrick J. Sullivan was born of Irish parents at Braddock, Pennsylvania, on St. Patrick's Day, 1894. His father died when he was two years old. His mother, burdened with a large family, no funds, and confronted with a period of long hospitalization for an illness, was compelled to place him in an orphanage, where he remained until he was fifteen. At that age he was able to rejoin his mother, and after working at various jobs, finally became a house painter, which is his trade today. He now lives in West Virginia with his wife and children.

It was during the depression that he found time for art and began to paint. He is self-taught. He paints with painstaking devotion over a long period of time, working the pigment into relief in many places on his canvas. His selection of color is subtle and restrained, and reflects the nature of his vocational background. These are his three completed pictures to date.

By the time the third painting arrived it was quite evident that the particular primitive quality which distinguished this artist's work was deeply embedded in his personality, and that, similarly, when the time came, the wide step from the shelter of carefully considered individual encouragement to a position before public appraisal would be made without disturbance to his untouched spirit.

SIDNEY JANIS

*169 MAN'S PROCRASTINATING PASTIME. 1936
Oil on canvas, 23¼ x 25¼ inches

*Note:* The artist has written elaborate explanations of the meaning of each picture, brief excerpts from which are included in Mr. Sidney Janis' essay, above.

*170 AN HISTORICAL EVENT. 1937
Oil on canvas, 20 x 24 inches

171 A RENDEZVOUS WITH THE SOUL. 1938
Oil on canvas, 25¼ x 25¼ inches

Nos. 169-171 lent by Sidney Janis, New York

# *Short Bibliography*

This list contains only the more important references. A more complete bibliography will be found in this museum's exhibition catalog, "American Folk Art," p.47-52.


## *General*

CAHILL, HOLGER. "American Folk Art." In: New York. Museum of Modern Art. *American Folk Art.* 1932. p.3-28.

## *Monographs on Individual Artists*

BRANCHARD, EMILE

Bourgeois Galleries, New York. *Exhibition of Paintings and Drawings by Emile Branchard.* Oct.11-Nov.1, 1919.
Foreword by Stephan Bourgeois.

———. *Exhibition of Paintings by Emile Branchard.* Mar.21-Apr.11, 1925.
Foreword by Stephan Bourgeois.

"Emile Pierre Branchard—Painter," *Index of Twentieth Century Artists,* 1937, v.4, p.375.

CANADE, VINCENT

CANADE, VINCENT. "Self-portrait," *Creative Art,* July, 1928, v.3, p.xxix.

EGLINGTON, GUY. "Vincent Canadé," *Creative Art,* July, 1928, v.3, p.xxx-xxxiv.

"Vincent Canadé—Painter," *Index of Twentieth Century Artists,* 1937, v.4, p.377-8.

HICKS, EDWARD

DRESSER, LOUISA. "The Peaceable Kingdom," *Worcester Art Museum Bulletin,* Apr., 1934, v.25, p.25-30.
Contains bibliography.

HICKS, EDWARD. *Memoirs of the Life and Religious Labors of E. Hicks.* Philadelphia, Merrihew and Thompson, 1851.

KANE, JOHN

"John Kane—Painter," *Index of Twentieth Century Artists*, Dec., 1935, v.3, p.213.

"Thumbs Up for John Kane," *Carnegie Magazine*, Nov., 1930, v.4, p. 181.

WATSON, FORBES. "The Carnegie International," *The Arts*, 1927, v.12, p.257-8.

PICKETT, JOSEPH

New York. Museum of Modern Art. *American Folk Art.* 1932. p.33-4.

B. N.

92 BRANCHARD *Winter Night*

96 BRANCHARD *The Struggle*

97 CANADÉ *Double Self Portrait*. 1923

98 CANADÉ *The Artist's Family*. About 1924

101 CAUCHON *The Red Surrey*

104 CERVANTEZ *Croquet Ground*. 1936

106 CERVANTEZ *Panhandle Lumber Company.* 1937

107 CERVANTEZ *Pink Oxalis on Stove.* 1937

111 CERVANTEZ *Cuates Privadas.* 1937

114 DALSON *Landscape*. 1936

Photograph by Charles Sheeler

118 HICKS *The Peaceable Kingdom*

119 HICKS *The Grave of William Penn.* 1847

122 HICKS *The Residence of David Twining in 1787*

128 HOYER *Inside a Barn*. 1937

132 HOYER *A Grazing Field*. 1937

133 HOYER *Forest Fire*. 1937

134 HUNT *Peter Hunt's Antique Shop*

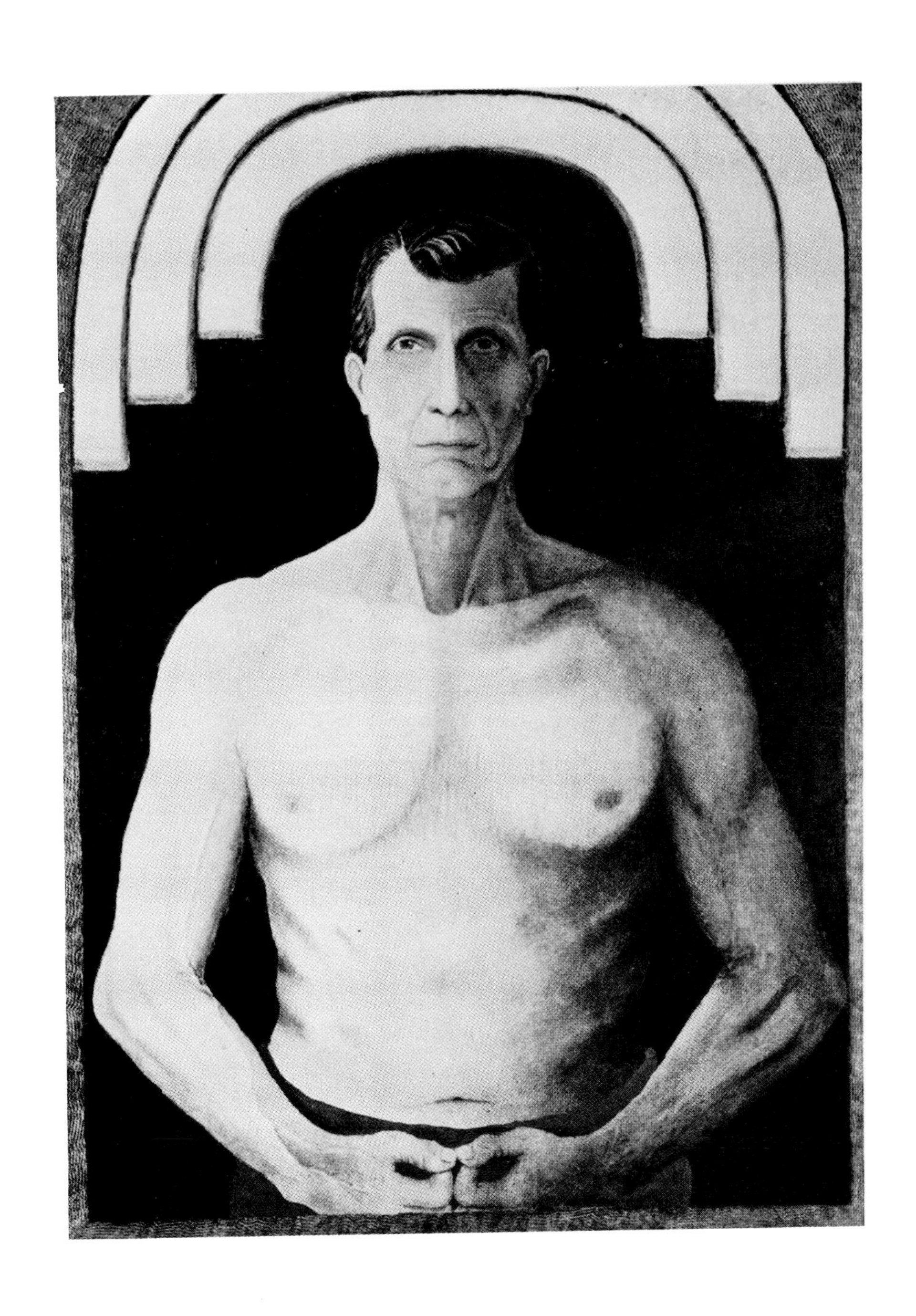

137 KANE *Self Portrait*. 1929

139 KANE *Brother Patrick in Uniform of the Black Watch*

143 KANE *Andrew Carnegie's Birthplace*

145 KANE *Old St. Patrick's*

147 KANE *Turtle Creek Valley*

148 KANE *Homestead*

149 KANE *Along the Susquehanna*

151 KANE *From My Studio Window.* 1932

153 KANE *Touching up*. About 1934

156 LEBDUSKA *Eve.* 1936

157 LEBDUSKA *The Monastery Farm, Rhode Island.* 1936

158 LEBDUSKA *Bohemian Kitchen*. 1936

160 LEBDUSKA *White Belt Cattle.* 1937

163 PICKETT *Washington under the Council Tree*. Probably 1914-1918

164 PICKETT *Coryell's Ferry, 1776, and Washington Taking Views.* Probably 1914-1918

165 PIPPIN *Shell Holes and Observation Balloon, Champagne Sector*

166 PIPPIN *The End of the War: Starting Home*

169 SULLIVAN *Man's Procrastinating Pastime.* 1936

170 SULLIVAN *An Historical Event*. 1937

# *Trustees*



# *Staff*

THIS REPRINTED EDITION WAS PRODUCED BY THE OFFSET PRINTING PROCESS. THE TEXT AND PLATES WERE PHOTOGRAPHED SEPARATELY FROM THE ORIGINAL VOLUME, AND THE PLATES RESCREENED. THE PAPER AND BINDING WERE SELECTED TO ENSURE THE LONG LIFE OF THIS LIBRARY GRADE EDITION.